GREAT CHRISTIANS

THE EARLY SAINTS

BOOK 1

by

Norman J. Bull, M.A.

Illustrated by R. G. Botting, A.R.C.A.

HULTON EDUCATIONAL PUBLICATIONS LTD

©
Norman J. Bull
1960

ISBN 0 7175 0426 3

First published 1960 *by*

HULTON EDUCATIONAL PUBLICATIONS LTD.,
Raans Road, Amersham, Bucks.

Reprinted 1962
Reprinted 1965
Reprinted 1970
Reprinted 1977
Printed in Malta by Interprint (Malta) Ltd

Other biographies of early saints and Christian heroes may be found in *Heroes of the Faith* by Norman J. Bull, published by HULTON EDUCATIONAL PUBLICATIONS. The time chart overleaf lists biographies appearing in this book and in *Heroes of the Faith:* dates given are in most cases the date of death, as birth dates are not always known.

Early Saints	A.D.	Heroes of the Faith
	30	Birthday of the Church
	35	Stephen, the First Martyr
	60	Andrew, Patron Saint of Scotland
	64	Peter the Leader
	64	Paul the Apostle
Ignatius, Martyr Bishop of Antioch	107	
Polycarp, Martyr Bishop of Smyrna	155	
	305	Alban, the First British Martyr
	305	George, the Patron Saint of England
	320	The Forty Martyrs of Sebaste
Ulfilas, Apostle of the Goths	383	
Telemachus, the Martyr Monk	391	
Martin of Tours	397	
Ambrose of Milan	397	
John Chrysostom	407	
Jerome of Bethlehem	420	
Augustine of Hippo	430	
Ninian, Apostle of Scotland	432	
	461	Patrick, Patron Saint of Ireland
	597	Columba, the Dove of the North
	601	David, Patron Saint of Wales
	604	Augustine, Apostle of England
Gregory the Great	604	
Oswald, the Martyr King	642	
Paulinus of York	644	
	651	Aidan, Apostle of Northumbria
Cedd and Chad, the Brother Bishops	664	
	672	
	680	Hilda (and Caedmon) of Whitby
Cuthbert of Lindisfarne	687	
Wilfrid, Apostle of Sussex	709	
	735	Bede, the Father of English History
Willibrord, Apostle of the Netherlands	739	
Boniface, Apostle of Germany	754	
Anskar, Apostle of the North	865	
	899	King Alfred the Great
	988	Dunstan of Glastonbury
Vladimir, Apostle of Russia	1015	

CONTENTS

1. Ignatius, the Martyr Bishop of Antioch

JESUS left the twelve Apostles to carry on His work on earth. They were to be His witnesses and to carry the Good News to men of all nations. They began their work in Jerusalem but it was not long before they were persecuted. Strict Jews attacked them for teaching that Jesus was the Son of God. A preacher named Stephen was stoned to death and the angry Jews determined to wipe out the new church. Some followers of Jesus went into hiding, others escaped from Jerusalem to neighbouring lands. Wherever they went they took their new faith

The Journey of St Ignatius from Antioch to Rome.

with them. It was in this way that the Gospel came to Antioch.

The great city of Antioch in Syria was called "Queen of the East". It was the third largest city in the whole Roman Empire, for it was a fine centre for government and trade. But it was an evil city, where people worshipped pagan idols and had bad ways. Many Jews lived there, true to God and faithful to their Law. They welcomed the refugees from Jerusalem and, when they heard about Jesus, some of them believed in Him. In the synagogues were some Greeks who were allowed to attend the services. Many of them listened eagerly to the preachers from Jerusalem and they were baptised. So a fine new church grew up at Antioch, and Barnabas was sent from Jerusalem to be its leader. He brought Paul from the city of Tarsus to help him and Antioch became Paul's headquarters. From it he set out on his missionary journeys and each time came back to report on his work. The pagans at Antioch gave these followers of Jesus a nickname which we still use today—"Christians".

The Apostle Peter visited Antioch too and was the first bishop of the church there. It was probably during Peter's stay at Antioch that a young man named Ignatius became a Christian. He had been born about A.D. 35 into a pagan home. Once he became a Christian he soon showed what a strong leader he was. The bishop who had been appointed by Peter died in A.D. 69 and Ignatius was chosen to be the new Bishop of Antioch. He was given a new 'Christian name'—'Theophorus', 'Bearer of God'.

It was hard to be a leader of the church in those times. Christians were hated and often attacked by pagans, by strict Jews and by Roman rulers. Only a man of great faith and courage could inspire his people to stand firm. Ignatius was like a rock to his church and feared nothing. When persecution broke out at Antioch in A.D. 107 he was at once arrested as leader of the Christians. He was brought before the Governor and ordered to worship the gods of Rome. Proudly he refused to betray Jesus and nothing could make him yield. Ignatius knew what the cost would be. He was sentenced to be taken to Rome and thrown to the lions in the arena.

It was a long journey to Rome. Ignatius was bound with chains and handed over to a company of ten soldiers. They were such cruel guards that he called them 'leopards'. "I am fighting with wild beasts all the way to Rome," he said. But he did not complain nor did he lose heart. We know exactly how he felt because he wrote letters on his journey which we can still read.

The first part of the journey was the long march by road from Antioch to Smyrna on the coast of the Aegean Sea. Here they stayed for a time and the bishops of all the churches round about came to greet Ignatius and to supply his needs. From Smyrna Ignatius wrote letters to these churches, praising them for their loyalty to Jesus. He told them to beware of false teachers and to obey their bishops in all things. He asked them, too, to send helpers to his own stricken church at Antioch. Then he wrote a letter to the Christians at Rome to make himself known to them. He was anxious that they should

do nothing to try to get him released. This letter was dated August 24th. "I am writing to all the churches," he said, "to tell them that I am going to my death willingly for the sake of Jesus. I beg you, do not try to save me. For if I die in the arena I shall go to God. I cannot order you as Peter and Paul did. They were Apostles; I am a convict in chains. But if you love me let me suffer that I may go to our Lord Jesus."

From Smyrna they travelled along the coast to Troas, the ancient city of Troy. While they waited for a ship Ignatius wrote a letter to the Christians at Smyrna and another to their bishop Polycarp, thanking them for being so kind to him and urging them to stand firm in their faith. His letter to Polycarp ended, "Our ship has now arrived and there is no time to write any more letters.

Please send messengers to the churches on the road ahead of me so that they may greet me just as you did. I send greetings to all my Christian friends in Smyrna. Farewell in the Lord, dear Polycarp."

The ship took them over the sea to Neapolis on the mainland of Greece. They marched overland to the west coast of Greece and there took ship to Italy. The long journey ended when at last they came to Rome. On the day of the Games, Ignatius was led into the great Colosseum, packed with a vast crowd. "Christians to the lions!" they yelled when the old bishop came into the arena. The hungry beasts were let loose and Ignatius met his death bravely, strong in faith and hope, praying for his enemies. That evening two loyal disciples of Ignatius, who had followed him all the way to Rome,

crept into the silent arena. They gathered up the remains of their beloved leader and took them back to Antioch for burial. Since that time, on February 1st every year, Christians have honoured the memory of Ignatius, the brave martyr Bishop of Antioch.

Questions and Things To Do

1. Find and read these passages in your Bible which remind us of Ignatius—

Stephen the first martyr	Acts 7. vv. 54–60
The church at Antioch	Acts 11. vv. 19–26
Martyr heroes of faith	Hebrews 11. vv. 32–40
The reward of the martyr	2 Timothy 4. vv. 7–8.

2. 'Martyr' comes from a Greek word meaning 'witness'. Some Christians like Ignatius were witnesses to Jesus in dying for their faith. Most Christians show their faith in their lives. In what ways can we be witnesses to Jesus in our daily lives?

3. Make your own map of the Roman world to show Antioch where Ignatius was Bishop and the journey he made to Rome.

4. Find in your Bible the book of Revelation 2. v. 10. Write out the last part of this verse in your notebook and learn it by heart.

5. Imagine you were one of the two Christians from Antioch who followed Ignatius to Rome, saw him martyred, and took back his remains to Antioch for burial. Write or give an account of your journey and what happened on the way.

6. Letter on an imitation scroll, in 'illuminated' writing if you can, these words of Ignatius from his letter to the church at Ephesus—

> ' Nothing is hidden from the Lord;
> Even our secrets are known to Him.
> We must therefore do all things
> As though He were dwelling within us.
> Then we shall be His temples,
> And He will be God in us.'

7. Draw the journey of Ignatius from Antioch to Rome in a series of pictures as a 'strip cartoon'. The scenes can be— his trial at Antioch; chained to the guards; with Polycarp at Smyrna; writing letters at the port of Troas; on board ship; in the arena at Rome.

8. Act the story of Polycarp coming to greet Ignatius at Smyrna. Make up in your own words the conversation they would have with each other.

9. An early Christian writer said—"The blood of the martyrs is the seed of the church." What do you think he meant by this?

10. Find hymns in your hymn-book which could be used for a service in memory of St. Ignatius, and read them through together. Suitable hymns would be—'The Son of God goes forth to war', 'Soldiers of Christ arise', 'He who would valiant be'. See if you can find others. Which do you think most suitable? Can you say why?

★

2. Polycarp, the Martyr Bishop of Smyrna

THE city of Smyrna, on the coast of Asia Minor, was a fine port in Roman times. It had grown rich through trade and even had its own coinage. The wealthy merchants lived in grand houses and the city had wonderful buildings. But the Christians of Smyrna were poor and were often attacked for refusing to worship the Roman gods and to sacrifice to the Emperor. It needed great courage to be a follower of Jesus in Smyrna for persecution might break out at any time. The bishop especially was in constant danger.

A little way south of Smyrna was the great city of Ephesus where John the Apostle lived in his old age. A young man named Polycarp heard him speaking of Jesus and he listened eagerly to John's memories of the things Jesus had said and done. Soon Polycarp was baptised and became a faithful disciple of John. He met other Apostles too and treasured their teachings. It was not long before John appointed him to be Bishop of the Church of Smyrna. It was a difficult and dangerous task, but no one could have been more fitted for it.

Bishop Polycarp was a great leader of the church. For nearly sixty years he worked at Smyrna, preaching the Good News of Jesus and guiding his people. His fame spread to other churches for he taught the true faith which he had heard from the Apostles themselves.

One day Polycarp heard the dreadful news that Ignatius, the brave bishop of Antioch, had been arrested and sentenced to die in the arena at Rome. He and his guards must pass through Smyrna and Polycarp hurried to greet his brother bishop and to bring him comfort. They became great friends and Polycarp never forgot the example Ignatius gave him of faith and courage. He wrote urgent letters to the churches in Greece through which Ignatius must pass so that they too could greet him and minister to him. They did this gladly and, when the sad news came that Ignatius had met a martyr's death, the Christians at Philippi decided to collect his letters. They wrote to Polycarp asking him to help them. We can still read his reply to them: "I am sending you the letters of Ignatius for which you asked. There are the two letters he wrote to us and also some others we have collected. I enclose them with this letter which faithful Crescens is bringing to you. You will find these letters of Ignatius full of fine Christian teaching and I know they will help you greatly. We treasure his memory too and hope you will send us anything further which you hear about that great man of God."

When he was an old man, Polycarp went on the long journey to Rome. He wanted to meet the bishop there and to discuss certain matters. For the churches of Asia had different customs from the churches in Europe. Many pagans in Rome were won to the church by the words of this saintly old man.

No sooner had Polycarp arrived back in Smyrna than persecution broke out against the Christians. It was the year A.D. 155 and the bishop was now an old man of 86 years. We can still read the story of his arrest and trial, written soon afterwards in a letter from his church. The Festival in honour of the Emperor was being held. It was a public holiday and the mob in the city wanted excitement. Suddenly someone raised the cry, " Down with the Christians! We want Polycarp!" The crowd raided his house but Polycarp was not there. His followers had forced him to go to a house on the outskirts of the town. A servant boy was tortured and made to reveal Polycarp's hiding-place. Mounted police were sent to arrest him. Polycarp refused to flee. He awaited them calmly and ordered food for them while he said his prayers. Then, seated on an ass, he was led back into the city.

The chief constable met him. He secretly admired Polycarp and wanted to save him. "Why don't you offer incense to the Emperor's statue?" he urged. "There's no harm in just saying 'Lord Caesar', is there?" Polycarp would not listen and was led into the stadium. As he entered he heard a voice saying, "Be strong, Polycarp! Play the man!" He was led up to the Roman Governor. He, too, wanted to save the aged bishop. "You are an old man, Polycarp. Why should you die in this way? Don't be obstinate. Make your oath to the Emperor, that's all, and then I can release you. Curse Christ and you are a free man!" Polycarp answered, "I have served Christ for eighty-six years. He has never done me wrong. How then can I wrong my King and blaspheme Him who has saved me?" Again and again the Governor urged him while the crowd yelled impatiently. Polycarp would not yield. "It is no use trying to make me worship the Emperor," he said. "Once and for all, I am a Christian. My King is in heaven. I cannot worship an earthly king." The Governor threatened him with the wild beasts and with fire, but it was useless.

Then the Governor gave up and sent his herald to proclaim to the crowd, "Polycarp has confessed to being a Christian!" The mob went mad with fury. "Bring on the lions!" they yelled. "Polycarp to the lions!" The president of the Festival refused, for the Games were ended. But the bloodthirsty mob were not going to be denied their sport. "Fire!" they shouted, "Polycarp to the flames!" Madly they gathered wood for a fire and heaped it round the aged bishop. Soon the flames were

leaping about him as he prayed but they did not seem to harm him. So a soldier was ordered to speed his death with a thrust of his dagger.

So died a brave follower of Jesus, faithful to the end. His example was never forgotten and still today, on January 26th, Christians remember Polycarp, the martyr Bishop of Smyrna.

Questions and Things To Do

1. Find and read these passages in your Bible which remind us of Polycarp—

The church at Smyrna	Revelation 2. vv. 8–10
Have no fear	1 Peter 3. vv. 14–17

Suffering for the Name of	
Christ	1 Peter 4. vv. 12–16
The reward of the martyr	Revelation 2. v. 10.

2. See that the cities of Ephesus and Smyrna are shown on your map of the Roman world. After Ephesus write 'John' in brackets and after Smyrna write 'Polycarp' in brackets to help you to remember where they worked. You can also add 'Ignatius' after 'Antioch' if you have not yet done so.

3. Imagine that you were one of the soldiers sent to arrest Polycarp and to guard him in the stadium. Write or give an account of all that happened. Describe Polycarp, how he behaved, and what you thought of his character.

4. Everyone in the Roman Empire had to sacrifice to the Emperor as a god. It was done simply by scattering a pinch of salt on the flame in front of his statue. It was really a test of loyalty to Rome, and most people did it without thinking. Jews and Christians would never do this. Why do you think they were so strict about it when other people did not mind doing it at all?

5. Act the story of the Governor trying to persuade Polycarp to deny Jesus and to worship the Emperor. Use your own words in telling what they said to each other.

6. Why do you think the Christians at Philippi wanted to make a collection of the letters of Ignatius?

7. Why do you think the martyrs were such brave men? Find in your Bible the book of Joshua 1. v. 9. What does this verse teach us about standing up for what we believe to be right? Make up a prayer asking God to give you this kind of courage.

8. Make up a service in honour of St. Polycarp. Choose a lesson and hymns which you think are most suitable. Choose a prayer or, better still, make up your own.

9. Polycarp became famous for handing on the true faith of the Apostles which is summed up in "The Apostles' Creed." Find this Creed and copy it into your notebook or letter it on an imitation scroll. Make sure you know it by heart.

10. Find in your hymn-book the hymns for saints. Choose the one which you think best describes St. Polycarp and read it through together in choral speaking.

★

3. Telemachus, the Martyr Monk

FOR another 150 years after the death of Polycarp, Christians were persecuted. Sometimes the Roman Emperor made an order against them. Sometimes priests of the pagan religions led riots against them. They were jealous because people no longer brought sacrifices to the temples of the ancient gods. But all this time the Church went on growing. It had fine leaders like Ignatius and Polycarp. The faith and courage of Christians, even when they suffered, made pagans admire them. So by A.D. 300 the Church had spread all over the Roman world. Then another Emperor made a bitter attack on Christians and many were put to death. St. George and St. Alban became martyrs at this time. But it was impossible to destroy the Church. In A.D. 312 Constantine became Emperor and one of the first things he did was to forbid attacks on Christians. "Christians and all other people must be free to worship as they wish," he ordered.

Now Christianity became the religion of the Roman Empire. Constantine made Sunday a public holiday so that Christians could go to church freely, and beautiful new churches were built. He made new laws to end cruelty to children and slaves and prisoners. Animals were to be treated kindly by drivers and carriers. The public Games, in which hundreds of men as well as animals were put to a cruel death, were to be stopped.

For a long time the Romans had enjoyed these Games. Every Roman city had its arena where the people gathered on holidays and festivals. It was shaped like a circle, covered with sand, and there were stone seats all round it. Just as we go to watch sports today, the Romans loved to go to watch the Games. But theirs were cruel and bloodthirsty. Sometimes animals fought against each other or even against men. Sometimes gladiators fought each other. These were specially-trained men, paid to fight each other with armour and swords or with nets and tridents. When one was beaten and the other was about to kill him, he could put his hand up to show he was defeated. If the crowd wanted him to be spared they waved handkerchiefs. But if they wanted him to die they all turned their thumbs downwards. Then the victor would kill him.

No wonder Constantine, the first Christian Emperor,

wanted to end these cruel Games. For a long time Christians had spoken against them and would never go near them. At last the law forbade them all over the Empire. But the Romans loved them too much to give them up all at once, and it seems that they were still held in some places. About A.D. 390 an Emperor named Honorius ruled over the Empire in the West. He was troubled because savage tribes were attacking the

Empire. The fierce Goths invaded Italy but the Roman army managed to defeat them and drive them back. Honorius was so delighted that he ordered public Games at Rome to celebrate his triumph. They were to be held in the great Colosseum which still stands today. This huge arena had tiers of seats round it for nearly 90,000 people. At last the great day came and the Colosseum was packed to the doors with an excited crowd eagerly waiting for the fighting to begin. It was January 1st in the year A.D. 391.

A certain monk named Telemachus was in Rome at that time. He came from the East where he lived alone as a hermit, devoting his life to prayer. He was not in Rome by chance. It seems he had heard of these terrible Games and was horrified by them. How could a Christian

21

Emperor and Christian people find sport and pleasure in watching men kill each other? He must end this cruel bloodshed and murder, he decided. So he had made the long journey to Rome to speak for God.

Telemachus was in the crowd at the Colosseum that day. He watched the strong, young gladiators march into the arena and up to the royal box where the Emperor sat in state. "Hail, Caesar!" they cried. "We, about to die, salute thee!" The huge crowd roared with pleasure and excitement. Suddenly they stopped. Telemachus had climbed over the stone wall round the arena and this strange figure was running towards the gladiators, shouting. What was it he was crying out? They could just hear: "Stop! In the name of Jesus Christ who died for men—stop!" Telemachus had thrust himself between the gladiators, separating them from each other. "The Games! The Games! Kill him! Kill him!" shouted the mob. One of the heartless gladiators pierced Telemachus with his sword and the holy man of the East fell dead upon the blood-stained sand.

A sudden silence filled the vast arena. The people there were not pagans as they had been in the old days. They called themselves Christians. They realised what they had done and they were ashamed. A monk, a holy man of God, had been murdered for their sport. Even the Emperor Honorius hung his head. Slowly the people began to make their way to the exits and silently they went back home. Before long the Colosseum was empty.

Never again were the Games held. The Emperor made a law banning them throughout the Empire. Everywhere

people were so shocked by the murder of Telemachus
that they never again clamoured for the blood sports of
the arena. Christians never forgot how he had given his
life to shame them into giving up their evil ways. Every
year the anniversary of that day, January 1st, is set
aside by many Christians to the memory of Telemachus
the monk. His sacrifice had done what laws could not
do. It had made Christians realise that every living person
is sacred and precious to God.

Questions and Things To Do

1. Find and read these passages in your Bible which remind us
   of Telemachus—

The commandment of Moses	Exodus 20. v. 13
The commandment of Jesus	St. Mark 12. v. 31
The greatest love	St. John 15. v. 13
The great commandment	Romans 13. vv. 8–10.

2. Telemachus showed in his death the great love of which Jesus spoke in St. John 15. v. 13. Write out this verse in your notebook or letter it on an imitation scroll, in 'illuminated' writing if you can. Make sure you know it by heart. Have you seen it written anywhere else? Look, for example, on your local war memorial.

3. Imagine you were there in the Colosseum at Rome on January 1st in A.D. 391. Write or give an account of everything that happened in the arena that day.

4. Find out all you can about monks, where and how they live, their daily life and work. Write an account of what you find with the title, 'A day in the life of a monk'. You can add your own drawings, with perhaps pictures of any monastery near your home.

5. Some orders of monks do fine work in the world among, for example, the poor and crippled and homeless. Others live all the time in their monastery. What differences are there between the life of a monk and the life of ordinary people? What do you think we can learn from them?

6. Find out all you can about the Emperor Constantine and write an account of his life. His mother St. Helena was British and Constantine lived for a time at York—'Eboracum', as the Romans called it. How did Constantine's new laws help the Christian church?

7. Pagan Romans took for granted and even enjoyed things like cruelty and slavery and bloodshed. Christianity ended such things. Why do you think this was? Why should Christians want to stop them?

8. In Africa recently there worked a great Christian missionary named Albert Schweitzer. He said that Christianity teaches "reverence for life". What do you think he meant by this?

9. Constantine made Sunday a public holiday each week. Why did Christians choose Sunday for their holy day instead of the Jewish Sabbath? What do you think we should do on Sunday?

10. Some people would like to have organised sports and games, such as cricket and football, on Sunday. Discuss or debate the advantages and disadvantages of this proposal.

★

4. Ulfilas, Apostle of the Goths

CONSTANTINE the Great, the first Christian Emperor, decided to build a new capital city. Rome was too far west to be a centre for the vast Roman Empire. He chose a place called Byzantium between the East and the West. There in A.D. 330 he built a wonderful new city, four times bigger than the old. It had great stone walls, fine streets, beautiful houses and churches, libraries and shops. Ships from all over the world could sail into the deep waters of its natural harbour called the Golden

Boundaries of the Roman
Empire under Constantine

Horn. The new imperial city was given a new name—
Constantinople.

It needed strong walls for all around it lived a fierce,
warlike tribe called the Goths. They had come long ago
from Scandinavia in the north. Some settled in the East
in what is now Russia, and are known as the East Goths
or 'OstroGoths'. Others settled in the West, in Europe,
and are called the 'West Goths' or 'VisiGoths'. These
VisiGoths lived by the River Danube. Constantine had
to fight their king Alaric. The Roman legions defeated
the fierce but undisciplined Goths and Constantine made

peace with them. Some Gothic boys were taken as hostages to Constantinople to make sure that the Goths kept the peace treaty. One of them was a boy named Ulfilas.

Ulfilas had been born in A.D. 311. His name in Gothic was really 'Wulfila' which means 'Little Wolf', for his parents hoped that he would become a great warrior. He grew up in his home in the woods where life was simple and savage. He loved best the evenings round the camp fire when warriors celebrated their victories in

songs of battle and of war. There too he heard songs and stories of the gods of his people—Tiw the god of war, Woden the chief of the gods, Thor the god of thunder and Balder the gentle sun god. Suddenly he was taken away from his home and sent to Constantinople.

Ulfilas had never seen a town before, let alone a wonderful city like this. We can imagine how amazed he must have been at this strange new life and how homesick he must have felt for his own home and his own people. But he soon found lots of things to interest and excite him, especially at school where he learnt to read and to write. There he learnt not only the Latin tongue of the Romans but also the Greek language. So he read books written in Greek. Homer's stories of the heroes of old would remind him of his own people and the Gothic warriors. But he also read something he had never heard of before—the story of Jesus Christ and His teaching. Here was a new kind of hero and it was not long before Ulfilas knew that he wanted to be a warrior of Jesus Christ.

Life in Constantinople was full of interest and comfort and Ulfilas could have stayed there in wealth and ease. But he had never forgotten his own people. He wanted to go back to them and to give them what Constantinople had given to him. In A.D. 341, when he was thirty years old, Ulfilas was made a bishop and set off back to his people.

The Goths welcomed him warmly and many listened gladly to the message of Jesus which Ulfilas brought them. But some of them would not hear of giving up the old gods and began to attack Ulfilas and his followers. He asked the Emperor if he might take them westwards over the River Danube so that they could settle there under the rule of Rome. They made their homes there in 348 A.D., in the country now called Roumania, living by their cattle and trade and no longer by war.

For over forty years Ulfilas worked as a missionary among his people. But he did more than preach. He soon realised that the Goths must have the Bible to read if they were to remain Christians. But there were great difficulties. The Goths could not read or write. There

was no Bible in Gothic. There was not even a Gothic language! All they had was a few crude letters called 'runes' for marking their possessions. Ulfilas started from the beginning. First, with his knowledge of Latin and Greek, he made a new Gothic alphabet. Then bit by bit he turned the Greek Bible into his new Gothic language. It took him years and years to do his great work. At last it was finished. The Bible was written in Gothic for his people to read. But it was not quite the whole Bible. Ulfilas deliberately left out of his Bible the Old Testament books of Kings, for they are full of stories of war and Ulfilas did not want to encourage his warlike people to start fighting again!

Today the Bible is printed in over a thousand different languages. For missionaries in modern times have done what Ulfilas was the very first missionary to do: translate the Bible into a language which no one knew how to write. Christian missionaries, trained by Ulfilas, travelled among the Goths, taking the Bible with them. At camp fires, instead of savage stories of the old gods being told, the story of Jesus was read instead. Through the work of one man the fierce Goths and the tribes of Teutons around them were turned from paganism to the Christian faith.

Ulfilas died in A.D. 383. Some years later his people revolted against the Roman Emperor. Under their king Alaric they invaded Italy. In A.D. 410 they entered Rome itself and sacked the great city. But the churches were spared and Christians who sheltered in them were unharmed. For, through the great work of Ulfilas, even these fierce warriors had been tamed by the Gospel of Jesus Christ.

Questions and Things To Do

1. Find and read these passages in your Bible which remind us of Ulfilas—

The command of Jesus	St. Matthew 28. vv. 19–20
The call of the missionary	St. Luke 10. vv. 1–9
Witnesses of Jesus	Acts 1. v. 8
Comfort of the Scriptures	Romans 15. vv. 4–6.

2. Make your own map of the Balkan Peninsula to show where Ulfilas did his work among the Goths.

3. See if you can read through and pick out the words in the Lord's Prayer in the Gothic Bible of Ulfilas. There is a

The Gothic Bible of Ulfilas

The Lord's Prayer

Atta (Father) unsar (our)

Thu in himinam,

Weihnai (hallowed be) namo thein.

Qimai (come) thiudinassus (kingdom) theins.

Wairthai (be done) wiljo theins,

Swe (as) in himina

Jah (also) ana airthai.

Hlaif (loaf) unsarana (our) thana (the) sinteinan
    (daily)

Gif uns himma daga (on this day).

Jah (and) aflet (let-off, forgive) uns

Thatei skulans sijaima (what owing we are)

Swaswe jah (as also)

Weis afletam thaim skulam (the debtors) unsaraim
    (our).

Jah ni briggais uns in fraistubnjai (temptation),

Ak (but) lausei uns af thamma ubilin;

Unte (for) theina ist thiudangardi (kingdom)

Jah mahts (might)

Jah wulthus (glory)

In aiwins (eternity).

Amen.

St. Matthew 6. vv. 9 = 13.

beautiful copy of his Bible at the University of Uppsala in Sweden. It was made by hand in the fifth century on parchment coloured purple. The letters are written in silver and gold. Letter the Lord's Prayer in Gothic or English on an imitation parchment with this 'illuminated' writing.

4. Use reference books to find out all you can about the Goths, the way they lived, dressed, ate, etc. Then write or give an account of 'A day in the Life of the Boy Ulfilas'.

5. Our days of the week got their names from the old pagan gods. Thus—

  Sunday   —day of the sun
  Monday   —day of the moon
  Tuesday   —day of Tew, god of darkness
  Wednesday—day of Woden, chief of the gods, and god
                   of war
  Thursday   —day of Thor, god of thunder
  Friday   —day of Frig, wife of Woden
  Saturday   —day of Saetere, god of hate

Copy this list into your notebook so that you will remember it.

6. Imagine you were Ulfilas as a boy taken to Constantinople as a hostage. Describe what you saw and how you. felt. Your reference books will help you to find out more about the Goths and also about the city of Constantinople.

7. Why was Ulfilas sure that the Goths needed the Bible if they were to remain Christians?

8. Write to the British & Foreign Bible Society, Queen Victoria Street, London, E.C.4, to get information on how the Bible is printed in different languages today.

9. In what ways does the Bible help us to live as Christians?

10. How do you think we can best use the Bible to learn more about God?

5. Martin of Tours

MARTIN the soldier-saint was born in the year A.D. 335 in Eastern Europe. His father, a Roman soldier, was stationed there in the country now called Hungary. Both his mother and father worshipped the pagan gods but it seems that Martin heard of Jesus Christ when he was still a boy. For one story says that when he was ten years old he ran away from home to become a monk. Of course he was much too young, and both his parents were angry. Martin's father wanted him to become a soldier too, and when he was fifteen he had to join the Roman army. But while he did his duties well, Martin knew in his heart that he would never be content with soldiering. A friend of Martin's wrote the story of his life which we can still read. He says that Martin was a kind officer, good to his men, and spending little of his pay so that he always had money to give away.

Martin moved from one garrison to another with his troops. When he was eighteen years old his regiment was posted to Amiens, a city of France, in the Roman province of Gaul. It was a hard winter that year and the troops were glad to be protected by their thick uniform. One morning they marched out of barracks into the crisp, frosty day. Martin was riding with his men, wearing his fine, warm military cloak. Suddenly he noticed a beggar, sitting by the city gate, blue with cold. He sat shivering, waiting for alms. Martin was full of pity for the old man and reached for his purse. But it

was empty. He had given away his last coin. What could he do to save the beggar from freezing to death? A sudden idea came to him and he leapt off his horse. He quickly drew out his sword and, snatching off his thick cloak, he sliced it in two. Gently he wrapped one part round the half-frozen beggar and then, remounting his horse, galloped after his men. Martin forgot all about the incident but that night it came back to him while he slept. In his dream he saw Jesus, surrounded by the angels, telling them how Martin had given Him his cloak. When he woke, Martin knew what he wanted to do with his life. Soon after, he was baptised into the Christian Church and obtained his release from the army. Now he would be a soldier of Jesus Christ for the rest of his life.

Martin knew that, if he was to be a good Christian soldier, his life must be just as stern and disciplined as it had been in the Roman army. He read the life of a famous monk named Antony and learnt from it how to fight the evil temptations inside himself. He knew he had to battle against pagan gods and evil ways, too, so he must be strong in spirit. He decided to become a hermit. He lived far from men but close to God. He slept on the ground, lived on roots and herbs, and spent his time in prayer. It was during this time that he became a friend of beast and birds for he was kind and tender, sharing his scanty food with them. That is why old paintings of Martin show him with a hare at his feet.

After spending some years as a hermit, Martin went to the city of Poitiers in France where the saintly Hilary was Bishop. Martin loved him dearly and wanted to be near him. There he founded the very first monastery in France. Later he moved to the banks of the River Loire, just outside the city of Tours, and founded a new monastery. He and his monks lived in caves cut in the cliffs. Their life was hard and simple for, like Martin, they were to be Christian soldiers. When they were trained, the monks went out in bands of twelve with a leader, like Jesus and His Apostles, and each band founded a new monastery. These monasteries were to be Christian 'garrisons' in enemy territory, for the people of Gaul were pagans. Martin's monks were to be missionaries, taking the light of the Gospel into the darkness.

Martin's fame spread and the people of Tours grew

to love this holy monk. In A.D. 371 their bishop died
and they had to choose another. There was no doubt
whom they wanted but would the humble monk be
willing to become a bishop? One story says that Martin
was tricked. A citizen of Tours went to the monastery
and pleaded with Martin to come to his sick wife. Martin
left his cave at once and when he reached the city was
seized by the people and forced to become their Bishop.

For nearly thirty years Martin worked as Bishop of
Tours. He still lived a hard life but no longer in his
monastery. He travelled ceaselessly through the countryside, preaching and teaching, caring for the poor and
needy. He had simple food and little sleep and at night
lay on the bare ground, wrapped only in his simple
cloak. His goodness and love helped Christians to follow

Jesus more faithfully. His self-sacrifice and his fearless teaching won pagans to the faith he preached and lived.

Martin hated cruelty of any kind and when some heretics were arrested by the Emperor he pleaded for them. He was very angry when he heard that the Emperor had put them to death and fearlessly said so. They were savage and cruel times and Martin's Christ-like character brought him the love of his people. He died in A.D. 397 but he was never forgotten. He was made patron saint of his own country, France, but his fame spread to other lands. In England many churches were named after him. The oldest was at Canterbury where there has been a Christian church dedicated to him for over 1,400 years. In London the famous church of St. Martin-in-the-Fields is named after him. Other churches, too, up and down our land remind us of him. November 11th was set aside in each year as the day dedicated to the memory of Martin, the great soldier of Christ and loving shepherd of His flock.

Questions and Things To Do

1. Find and read these passages in your Bible which remind us of Martin—

Fight the good fight	1 Timothy 6. vv. 11–12
Christian soldiers	2 Timothy 2. vv. 3–4
The office of a bishop	Titus 1. vv. 7–9.

2. In your Bible find Ephesians 6. vv. 13–17. They describe the armour of a Roman soldier and what each part stands for

in the Christian life. Draw a Roman soldier; name on your drawing each piece of armour and what it represents.

3. Martin believed that to be a good Christian he must live a hard and strict life. What do you think about this? In what ways do you think a Christian must discipline himself?

4. Look up these verses in your Bible—St. Matthew 25. vv. 31–45; St. Mark 9. v. 41. In what way do you think they inspired Martin to treat the beggar as he did?

5. Imagine you were one of Martin's soldiers that day when he shared his cloak with a beggar. Describe what happened and what you and the other soldiers thought about your officer.

6. Martin gave away all he could to others, denying himself. We call this 'charity', an old word for 'love'. How do you think Christians should use their money? How much should we give to the church and to the needs of others?

7. Find in your hymn-book hymns which describe us as being Christian soldiers, such as 'Onward Christian soldiers', 'Soldiers of Christ arise'. Choose the one you think best fits St. Martin. Read it together in choral speaking or write out the most suitable verses in your notebook. Can you say why you chose it? If it is not familiar, you could learn it to use in school assembly.

8. If there is any church near you named after Martin, visit it; find out all you can about it, and write a 'history' of it. If there is none, make a 'history' of either St. Martin's Church, Canterbury, or St. Martin-in-the-Fields, London. You will need to use reference books for this.

9. Martin was very strict with his monks but he did allow them to copy manuscripts—the only books in those days. Choose your favourite text or psalm, especially one that you think

Martin might have liked, and letter it in 'illuminated writing' like one of his monks.

10. It was the monks, like those trained by Martin, who won the pagan tribes which had over-run Europe to Christianity. Why do you think monks made such good missionaries? Why was a monastery so helpful in this work?

★

6. Ambrose of Milan

AMBROSE was born in the year A.D. 339 at a place called Trier in France, for his father was the Governor of France, or Gaul as the Romans called it. He was rich and important and Ambrose grew up in a happy and wealthy home. He had a brother and sister whom he loved dearly all his life. When he was ten years old his father died and his mother went back to live in her old home near Rome. There Ambrose grew up into a fine young man. He studied law and soon showed himself to be wise as well as clever and a fine speaker. When he had finished his studies, he was appointed to a government post like his father before him. So great was his ability that in A.D. 370 he was made Governor of Northern Italy. His residence was at the city of Milan which had become even as important as Rome itself. For Milan was much nearer to the northern frontiers of the Empire

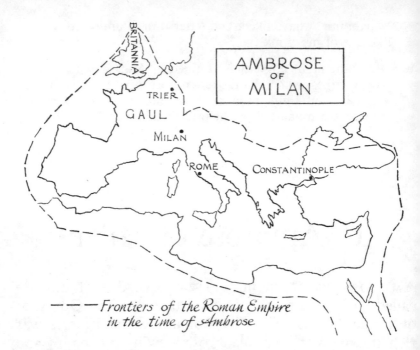

—————— *Frontiers of the Roman Empire*
in the time of Ambrose

where fierce tribes were always threatening. The Emperor often lived at Milan instead of Rome so Ambrose held a very important post. He ruled wisely and firmly and the people of Milan soon came to love him for he was always just.

Four years later the Bishop of Milan died and the people had to choose someone to succeed him. There was a sad quarrel in the church at that time, and there were two different parties. One group taught that Jesus was a very fine Man but that He was not truly God. They were called 'Arians' after their leader, Arius. Other Christians opposed them for they saw how dangerous and untrue this teaching was. They were called the 'orthodox', or 'right believing' party. For they taught the true faith of the whole Church. The old Bishop of Milan had been an Arian and his followers hoped to choose another Arian for bishop. The other party of course wanted an orthodox bishop.

When the day came for the election the cathedral at Milan was packed to the doors. Ambrose the Governor was there, for a quarrel might break out between the two parties and turn into a riot. He stood up to address the people and to bid them choose their bishop peacefully. As he waited for silence a child cried out—"Ambrose, Bishop!" Suddenly everyone took up the cry—"Ambrose for Bishop!" The Governor tried to silence them but they went on shouting, "Ambrose for Bishop!" Finally

he had to give in. At that time he was undergoing the long preparation for baptism. But the people would not wait and within a week he was baptised and made Bishop of Milan.

Ambrose ruled over the church wisely. His fine character and his Roman training in government made him a great leader of the church in Italy. He lived a simple and strict life and set a splendid example to others. He gave all his money to his brother to use for charity. He did all he could to help the building of monasteries where men lived together in poverty, devoting themselves to the service of God and men. His sister became a nun.

Because he feared God, Ambrose feared no one else and stood up even to rulers when they did wrong. The Roman Empire was now divided into two parts, East and West. In the West the Empress Justina ruled for her young son. She was an Arian and soon hated Ambrose who taught the true orthodox faith of the Church. She had many Goths serving as soldiers in her army and they were Arian Christian too. She demanded a church in Milan for their use but Ambrose refused. She sent her soldiers to surround the church she wanted but Ambrose filled it with his followers and taught them new hymns which he himself had written. Even the Empress dare not send her soldiers to attack the congregation and she had to give in. The next year she ordered Ambrose to argue against an Arian bishop in her own court but again he refused. "The Empress is a member of the Church, not lord over it," he said. Justina died not long after and the false, Arian teaching

A HYMN OF PRAISE

(Written by Ambrose)

Infinite God, to Thee we raise
Our hearts in solemn songs of praise;
By all Thy works on earth adored,
We worship Thee, the common Lord;
The everlasting Father own,
And bow our souls before Thy throne.

Thee all the choir of angels sings,
The Lord of hosts, the King of Kings
Cherubs proclaim Thy praise aloud,
And seraphs shout the Triune God;
And 'Holy, Holy, Holy' cry,
Thy glory fills both earth and sky.

Father of endless majesty,
All might and love they render Thee;
Thy true and only Son adore,
The same in dignity and power;
And God the Holy Ghost declare,
Thy saints' eternal Comforter.

Translated by Charles Wesley

Cherubs, seraphs—angels
Triune—three in one, the Holy Trinity
Comforter—Strengthener

about Jesus soon died out. Ambrose saved the true Christian faith by his courage.

It was like that, too, with the Emperor of the East named Theodosius. He was a sincere Christian but his fiery temper sometimes made him do terrible things. Once when he was in Milan he came to the cathedral for the service of the bread and wine. He came up to the altar to make his offering. But instead of returning to his seat he stayed there in the sanctuary, the holiest part of the church. Ambrose sent him a message telling him to go back to his place in the congregation. The Emperor had to obey. "Now I know the difference between a Bishop and an Emperor!" he said afterwards.

Some time later Theodosius did a dreadful deed. His officer in the city of Thessalonica in the East arrested a famous charioteer for a crime he had committed. The people were very angry for they were looking forward to the Games. There was a riot and the officer was killed. The Emperor was furious. "They shall have their Games," he said, grimly. The great day came, the arena was packed and the doors were locked. The Emperor had sent his soldiers in among the crowd. At the signal they drew out their swords. Seven thousand people died in a horrible massacre. A few months later the Emperor came to Milan and on Christmas Day went to the Cathedral for Holy Communion. Ambrose met him at the door. "You cannot receive the bread and wine till you have done penance for your awful deed," he said. Theodosius realised then how great was his sin. Only after penance was he admitted to the church.

Ambrose was a great teacher and preacher. In his sermons and hymns and books he proclaimed the true faith. When he died in A.D. 397 he was never forgotten. December 7th was set aside each year for Christians to remember and to thank God for Ambrose of Milan, a great leader of the Church.

Questions and Things To Do

1. Find and read these passages in your Bible which remind us of Ambrose—

    The Christian preacher   Colossians 3. vv. 16–17
    The Christian teacher   2 Timothy 4. vv. 1–5
    The Christian leader   Titus 1. vv. 7–9.

2. Write your own account of the life of Ambrose. You can

do this in your notebook or make a special booklet for this purpose. See if you can find more details about him in reference books.

3. Add to your story of Ambrose's life a map to show Italy in his time and the borders of the Roman Empire.

4. Make your own copy of the hymn of Ambrose and read it together in choral speaking. It would be a fine hymn to learn for use in school assembly.

5. You have read in this story three exciting scenes in the life of Ambrose. Imagine you were a reporter at one of these scenes and write an account of it for your paper (say, 'The Milan Express').

6. 'Ambrosia' in ancient times meant 'the food of the gods'. So it came to be used of anything sweet and delightful to taste, for example, honey. Perhaps this is why the Italian painters often included a beehive in their pictures of Ambrose. Sometimes they painted an angel whispering in his ear. Make your own painting or drawing of him, or draw the story of his life in a series of pictures as a ' strip cartoon'.

7. Ambrose is the patron saint of domestic animals. Make up a prayer for his festival day asking that we may care for our pets and be kind to all animals.

8. The service of bread and wine is known as Holy Communion or The Lord's Supper. It comes to us from Jesus Himself. Read what Jesus did at the Last Supper in St. Luke 22. vv. 14–20. Find out about this service in your own church, what it is called, when it is held, what happens, and who may take part in it. Write or give an account of what you find.

9. Ambrose made the Emperor do penance for his sin. This was very strict in those days. The penitent had to lie on the

floor of the church, dressed in sackcloth, and mourn his sin. Today we confess our sins in church in the 'General Confession'. Find this and read it through together, or make up your own prayer of confession to God.

10. Do you think Ambrose was right in standing up to the Emperor? What place do you think a ruler should have in the church of his land? What can we learn from the example of our own Queen?

★

7. Augustine of Hippo

WHEN Bishop Ambrose spoke to the people in Milan Cathedral, a young man sat listening to him eagerly. His name was Augustine and he came from Tagaste in North Africa where he had been born in A.D. 354. His father was a pagan but his mother, Monica, was a Christian and she had great hopes for her son. He began the preparation for baptism, but when he went to university in the city of Carthage nearby, he gave up his Christian training. Many years later he wrote the story of his life and in it he tells about his childhood and youth. He remembered how he and his gang had raided the orchard of a neighbour and stolen his pears. They were not even ripe and the lads only took nibbles before throwing them to the pigs. It was such a stupid thing to do but Augustine could see later that many things he

had done had been silly and sometimes evil. He was very clever at the university and studied to become a lawyer. But he wasted much of his time in idleness and folly. He followed strange religions but his mother went on praying that one day he would find real truth and wisdom in Jesus Christ.

Augustine went to live and teach in Rome and then became a professor at Milan. Here he listened to the sermons of Ambrose and was very attracted by the wisdom and by the pure life of the great Christian leader. Ambrose seemed to have the answers to the problems that had always troubled Augustine. Could Christianity be the truth? One day Augustine sat in a garden at Milan thinking. Two words kept running through his mind, "Tolle, lege"—"take up, read". He looked around him and saw on a bench a scroll. It was part of the New Testament. He began to read it and suddenly felt that his long struggle was over. Here was the truth and he gave himself to it with a full heart.

How happy Monica was that day before Easter in the year A.D. 387 as she watched Bishop Ambrose baptising her son. She died soon after but she had lived long enough to see all her prayers answered. Augustine went back to North Africa and lived with some Christian friends in a monastery at his home town of Tagaste, studying and writing. He became a priest and, though he still lived in his monastery, his influence spread. In 395 A.D. he was made Bishop of the town of Hippo and lived

there for over thirty years, a great shepherd of the flock of Christ.

Augustine lived in troubled times. Fierce pagan tribes were battering at the frontiers of the Roman Empire and breaking them down. In A.D. 410 the warlike Goths over-ran Italy and sacked the great city of Rome. I seemed like the end of the world. "Why does God allow this to happen?" Christians lamented. Augustine answered them in his greatest book of all called 'The City of God'. Empires rise and fall, he said, because they are made by greed and conquest. But the Church of God is an eternal city and His kingdom can never fall. Even as Augustine lay dying at his home in Hippo other fierce barbarians, the Vandals, were hammering at the gates of his city. But Augustine's great faith comforted many Christians and helped the Church to go out and win these barbarians to Jesus Christ.

There were enemies within the Church as well. When Christians had been persecuted, many years before, some of them had been so afraid that they had denied Jesus and worshipped the pagan gods. When persecution ended they wanted to come back to the Church again. Wise bishops welcomed them back, if they were truly sorry. But some proud members of the Church would not agree and they went off and started a separate church of their own. They said that their church was the true one for there were no sinners in it who had denied Jesus. All their members were holy, they said proudly. Augustine was horrified. He knew that the Church is holy because Jesus founded it. But that did not mean that everyone in it was holy. The Church is like a hospital. For a hospital is full of sick people who go there for healing. The Church is full of people who enter it to seek God's healing power for their souls. Augustine said that the Church is like an ark or a ship, a place of safety from the dangerous waters of the world. His teaching about the Church saved it from any more divisions.

Augustine found another enemy within the Church. His name was Pelagius and he came from Britain where he was a monk. Pelagius went to Rome and taught there. When Rome was taken by the Goths he went to North Africa. Augustine was shocked by his teaching. Pelagius taught that everyone is born good and is free to choose good or evil. It was easy for Pelagius to believe this. He had lived quietly in a monastery all his life and had never been really tempted to do wrong. But Augustine had never forgotten how he had stolen the useless pears when he was a boy, just out of sheer devilment. He had known many temptations all his life and he had done great wrong. It was God who had made him see the light and turn from his evil ways, not his own goodness. So Augustine began to speak against the teaching of Pelagius. He taught that it is only through the grace or power of God that we can live good lives. The Church realised that he was right and the teaching of Pelagius was condemned.

In such ways Augustine fought as a doughty champion of the Church. He died in A.D. 430 but he still spoke to Christians through his many great writings. He was made one of the four great 'Doctors' or 'Teachers' of the Church, for his teachings guided it for many centuries to come. August 28th was set aside as the day in each year on which Christians should remember Augustine of Hippo, a great leader and teacher of the Church of God.

Questions and Things To Do

1. Find and read in your Bible these passages which remind us of Augustine of Hippo—

The Church is like a body	1 Corinthians 12. vv. 12–14
The Church is one	Ephesians 4. vv. 4–6
The gift of God's grace	Ephesians 2. v. 8
The power of grace	Philippians 4. v. 13
Strong in grace	2 Timothy 2. v. 1.

A PRAYER OF AUGUSTINE

O Thou who art
The light of the minds that know Thee,
The life of the souls that love Thee,
The strength of the wills that serve Thee;
Help us
So to know Thee that we may truly love Thee,
So to love Thee that we may fully serve Thee,
Whom to serve is perfect freedom.
Through Jesus Christ our Lord.

Amen.

2. Write your own story of Augustine, using reference books to find out all you can and making a booklet about him.

3. Add to your account of Augustine's life a map of North Africa and Italy to show the places where he lived and worked.

4. You could illustrate your story of Augustine with your own drawings of important events in his life. You may also find pictures of the remains of Roman cities in North Africa to add to it.

5. Copy out the fine prayer of Augustine on this page and add it to your booklet. You should learn it by heart so that you can use it in your own prayers and in school assembly.

6. Augustine said that the Church is like a ship. That is why the body of every church is called the 'nave', for the Roman word *navis* means a ship. The nave is like an over-turned ship, protecting God's people. Make a plan of your own church and write in the names given to each part, including

of course the nave. You can fix your plan in your booklet on Augustine.

7. For what reasons could we say that the Church is like a hospital for the sick?

8. Here are some famous words of Augustine: "Thou hast made us for Thyself, and our hearts are restless till they rest in Thee." Copy them into your booklet or notebook and see if you can learn them by heart.

9. Pelagius taught that everyone is born good and that we are free to do good or evil. God only helps us when we have decided to do good. Why did this seem so wrong to Augustine? What did he say in answer to Pelagius? What is your own experience?

10. You have read in this story of two great books written by Augustine, 'The City of God' and 'The Confessions'. It is in 'The Confessions' that he tells the story of the pears. See if you can borrow a copy of this book from your library and read this story. You will find it in chapter 2. What did Augustine learn from it about the badness inside himself? What can we learn from it?

★

8. Jerome of Bethlehem

JEROME was born in A.D. 342 near the town of Aquileia in the far north of Italy. His parents were well-to-do Christians and when Jerome was seventeen years old he went to Rome to study. The Church was strong in Rome and its Bishop was becoming important. But many of the people of Rome were still pagans and they lived for wealth and comfort. The Church was no longer persecuted and so it was easy to be a Christian. Some members of the Church began to live like the pagans in luxury and gaiety. Jerome was shocked by their easy ways for he believed that a Christian should live a strict, disciplined life. While he was in Rome he was baptised and then he travelled for a time in Gaul. He returned to Italy and settled near his home with some friends. They planned to live strictly and to study the Bible. But Jerome was a quarrelsome person and they soon parted.

Jerome set off to visit Palestine and on the way stopped

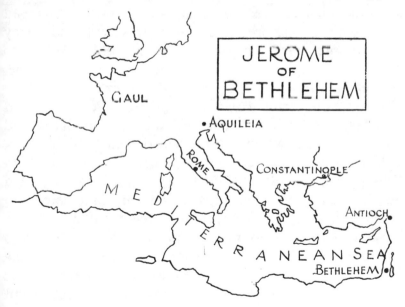

JEROME
OF
BETHLEHEM

GAUL

• AQUILEIA

ROME

CONSTANTINOPLE

M E D I T E R R A N E A N   S E A

ANTIOCH

BETHLEHEM

at Antioch in Syria. Here he had a dream which changed his whole life. He dreamed that he was being judged by God for preferring other books to the Bible. When he awoke he determined to study nothing but the Bible. He left the city and went off into the desert alone. There he lived as a hermit for several years, devoting himself to prayer and study. His life was terribly hard and strict. He went without food and denied himself sleep. Under the glaring sun his body became as black as an Ethiopian's, he said. All through his life Jerome treated his body like this. Perhaps it was this that helped to make him so quarrelsome and ill-tempered.

While Jerome lived near Antioch he met a Jew who had become a Christian. From him Jerome learnt the Hebrew language. This was to make him an even better scholar of the Bible. For of course the Old Testament had been written in Hebrew. After nearly five years in the desert Jerome went back to Antioch and then on to Constantinople where there were fine Christian scholars and manuscripts. Then he returned to Rome.

The Bishop of Rome at that time was named Damasus. He soon realised what an excellent scholar Jerome was and made him his secretary. Even in Rome, with all its wealth and gaiety, Jerome lived a stern life and wore the rough garment he used in the desert. In his sermons he bitterly attacked Christians who wore fine clothes and lived in luxury. Bishop Damasus encouraged him to go on with his Bible studies. But when Damasus died, Jerome had made so many enemies in Rome that he determined to leave. In A.D. 386 he finally settled at Bethlehem where he lived for the rest of his life.

Jerome founded a monastery at Bethlehem and some ladies from Rome set up a nunnery nearby. Here Jerome devoted himself to the two things he loved best—a strict life and study. For thirty-four years he worked in his cell on a new Latin Bible. There was already a Latin Bible used throughout the Church but Jerome had discovered how bad it was. The Old Testament had been first written in Hebrew and the New Testament in Greek. Jerome knew both these languages and he wanted to make a Latin Bible that was a true one, not full of mistakes like the one people used. He was never satisfied with his work and he went over it again and again. At last in A.D. 404 it was finished. He had translated the whole Bible into Latin. Though it was a new Bible it was really the oldest, for it was translated

from the very earliest manuscripts. Latin was the Roman language and now everyone could read the Bible.

At first many people did not like Jerome's Bible. It was often different from the one they were used to. Jerome expected this and he wrote in the preface of his Bible—"Both clever and ignorant people will call me a forger and a blasphemer for daring to change and to correct the Bible they know." But what mattered was the truth of his Bible. Scholars like Augustine of Hippo saw at once what a wonderful Bible it was and slowly others began to get used to it. In time it grew so popular that it became the Bible of the whole Church in the West.

Jerome's Bible is known as the 'Vulgate'. The Latin word *vulgatus* means 'made known to the people', and the Vulgate was the people's Bible of Europe all through the Middle Ages. Then people began to want the Bible in English. The Roman Catholic Church had always used the Vulgate as their Bible and in 1609 it was turned into English. Roman Catholics still use this translation, so that to this very day Jerome's Bible is read in churches Sunday by Sunday. But the Vulgate was used in making other English Bibles, too, for it was the best Latin Bible, going back to the earliest manuscripts. We can see then how great Jerome's work was.

In his little cell at Bethlehem Jerome wrote many other books on the Bible. He was the greatest scholar of the Church and his books helped Christians to understand and to teach the Scriptures. He wrote many letters, too, for his advice and help were wanted on the problems of the Church. He wrote bitter letters against false teachers like Pelagius, for he was still very quarrelsome. But we can understand that, because his life was so hard and strict. He always denied himself and he tried to persuade others to live as he did.

Jerome died in A.D. 420 and was made a 'Doctor' or 'Teacher' of the Church. Artists always pictured him with a lion, for it was said that when he was a hermit a lion was his friend and companion. September 30th was set aside to his memory. But our English Bible is the best memorial we have of Jerome of Bethlehem, the great Christian monk and scholar.

Questions and Things To Do

1. Find and read these passages in your Bible which remind us of Jerome—

The lamp of Scripture	Psalm 119. vv. 103–105
Strength from the Scriptures	Romans 15. v. 4
Christian discipline	1 Corinthians 9. vv. 24–27
The hard life	2 Timothy 2. v. 3.

2. Write your own account of the life and work of Jerome in your notebook or in a special booklet.

3. Add to your story of Jerome a map to show the places where he lived and worked.

4. Illustrate your story of Jerome with your own drawings. You could draw the story of his life in a series of pictures as a strip cartoon. See if you can also find any old pictures of Jerome to copy and pictures of Rome or Bethlehem to add to your notebook or booklet. If you draw Jerome, do not forget the lion which is always shown in pictures of him.

5. The strict way of life which Jerome lived is called 'asceticism'. This comes from a Greek word meaning 'exercised' or 'disciplined'. Paul had watched the Greek athletes exercising and said that Christians should live strictly like athletes (see 1 Corinthians 9. vv. 24–27). Jerome followed his advice. In what ways do you think Christians should discipline themselves?

6. See if you can borrow a copy of the Bible of the Roman Catholic Church which is translated from Jerome's Latin Bible. Find in it some passages you know well and compare them with the same passages in your own Bible. See what differences you can find.

7. Answer these questions in your notebook: Why was Jerome's Latin Bible such a good one? Why is it called the Vulgate?

8. A group of ladies from Rome, led by Jerome's friend Paula, set up a nunnery at Bethlehem. There, as well as at Jerome's monastery, pilgrims to the Holy Land were welcomed.

Imagine you **were** one of these pilgrims. Write or give an account of your journey, of the monastery and nunnery at Bethlehem, and of Jerome the monk.

9. Jerome lived a very lonely life, first as a hermit and then as a monk. Why did he do this? How did he serve God living alone? How can we serve God living with others?

10. Jerome had to write every word of his books and for centuries the Bible had to be written by hand as there were no printing-presses. Letter, in illuminated writing if you can, one of the passages above as the monks used to do.

★

9. John Chrysostom

JOHN was born at Antioch in the year A.D. 347 and was brought up by his mother in the Christian faith. He studied law and soon showed himself to be a wonderful speaker. He could have become very rich and famous as a lawyer. But when he was baptised at the age of twenty-three years he gave up the study of law. Like Jerome, he wanted to live a strict life as a monk. But his mother was now a widow and pleaded with him to stay with her. So he lived at home, but even there he kept very strict rules for food and sleep and study. When she died he left Antioch and, like Jerome, went out to live in the desert as a hermit. His life was very hard. For eight years he denied himself and treated his body

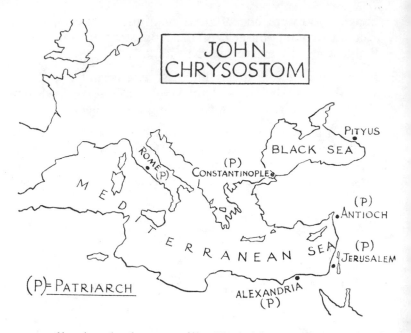

so cruelly that he became ill. He had to return to Antioch where he became a priest and a famous preacher. He had not lost his gift for public speaking. His sermons were so wonderful that John was given a nickname—'Chrysostom', a Greek word which means 'Golden-mouthed'.

John Chrysostom was well known at Antioch and he soon became a great leader of the people by his preaching. He taught the true faith and showed how Christians should live the good life. He spoke plainly when he felt it was needed. Antioch was a rich town and many pagans lived there. Christians were tempted to live as they did, thinking only of money and pleasure, comfort and ease. Chrysostom spoke sternly to his congregations. He

taught them that there were more important things in
life than getting money. He taught the rich to care for
the poor. He bade husbands and wives be kind and
thoughtful to each other. The Christians of Antioch
did not mind the hard things Chrysostom said in his
sermons for they knew him well and loved him as their
father in God.

For twelve years John Chrysostom lived at Antioch,
preaching and writing books. It was his own town and
he was very happy there. But he was taken from Antioch.
By now the Roman Empire had been divided into two
parts, the East and the West. The Emperor of the East
had his capital at the great city of Constantinople. As

a result, the Bishop of Constantinople became very important. But in the East the Emperor always took a leading part in Church affairs and chose bishops. In A.D. 398 the Bishop of Constantinople died. The Emperor chose the famous John to be the new bishop. But he knew that John loved his own city of Antioch and would not want to leave it. So John was made a prisoner, taken to Constantinople and made Bishop there against his will. It was the last thing he wanted. But once he had been made Bishop he accepted his new work and put his whole heart into leading his church.

John began to preach at Constantinople just as he had done at Antioch. Life there was even more splendid and gay. He spoke sternly to his congregations. He criticised the rich for loving money and not caring for the poor. He spoke against the women for their love of finery and their extravagance. He was very strict with the priests of his church too. John still lived the hard and severe life of the monk and expected them to do the same. He was not a wise leader of the Church as Ambrose was. He wanted to make the life of the city purer and to make Christians live simply, sharing their possessions as the first Christians had done. But he was too harsh. He did not care how he hurt the feelings of others. The Bishop before him had been too easy-going but John was too strict. Soon he made many enemies in Constantinople among the rich and important people. He had few friends except among the common folk.

The Emperor was a weak ruler but his wife was powerful. She soon grew to hate John Chrysostom for she felt he was criticising her. When he spoke against her in his sermons she determined to get rid of him. She persuaded the Bishop of Alexandria to help her, for he was jealous of John. He called a meeting at which all sorts of charges were made against John. He was condemned and sent into exile. But the common people demanded that their Bishop should be brought back. The Empress was frightened by an earthquake which shook the city and she gave in. Chrysostom returned to Constantinople and there was great rejoicing.

Soon the Empress was again furious with the Bishop. She had a beautiful silver statue of herself put up right in front of the great church of St. Sophia. John criticised her in public and she decided this time she would stand him no longer. Again she got the Bishop of Alexandria to condemn him. John was at first made a prisoner in his own house; then he was sent into exile. He was made to live in a village far away in the mountains of Taurus. His life was hard and cruel but he worked there for three years. His fame had spread throughout the Church and he had great influence through his letters. Many bishops, especially in the West, knew that a great wrong had been done. The Bishop of Rome said that John was still Bishop of Constantinople. He wrote to the Bishop of Alexandria condemning him for the evil he had done.

· The Empress and her friends were angered that John should still have such influence. They wanted him dead but they dare not kill him. Instead they ordered the guards to take him to a fortress at Pityus on the border

of the Empire near the Black Sea. They were to give him no rest. The dreadful journey went on for three months, through burning sun and torrents of rain. John Chrysostom was then sixty years old, worn out by his strict life. Day after day, with little food or rest, he was pushed on till at last he fell by the roadside. His last prayer was "Glory to God for all things". So he died, as his enemies intended he should. Thirty years later his body was brought back to Constantinople and buried in honour. January 27th was set aside as the festival day of John the Golden-mouthed, Bishop and saint of the Church of God.

A PRAYER OF JOHN CHRYSOSTOM

Almighty God
Who hast given us grace
At this time
With one accord
To make our common supplication unto Thee;
And dost promise
That when two or three are gathered together
In Thy name
Thou wilt grant their requests:
Fulfil, now, O Lord,
The desires and petitions of Thy servants,
As may be most expedient for them;
Granting us
In this world knowledge of Thy truth,
And in the world to come life everlasting.

Amen

Questions and Things To Do

1. Find and read in your Bible these passages which remind us of John Chrysostom—

The preacher of good tidings	Isaiah 52. v. 7
Jesus preaching at Nazareth	St. Luke 4. vv. 16–21
The work of the preacher	Romans 10. vv. 13–15
The preacher's message	1 Corinthians 2. vv. 2–4

2. Write your own story of the life of John Chrysostom either

in your notebook or in a special booklet. You can use reference books to find out more about him.

3. Make your own map of the Roman world to show where John Chrysostom lived and worked and add it to your account of his life.

4. By now there were many Bishops in the Roman Empire. Five of them had become more important than all the others. They were the Bishops of Rome, Alexandria, Antioch, Constantinople and Jerusalem. Each of these leading bishops was called a 'Patriarch', from the Greek words meaning 'Father-ruler'. Mark on your map these five places. You can add 'P' after each in brackets to show that their Bishops were Patriarchs.

5. A Prayer Book was made at Constantinople for use in the services there. It was named after John Chrysostom. In it is found a very famous prayer which is thought to have been written by him. Copy out this prayer in your notebook or booklet. It is a fine prayer to learn by heart.

6. Compare the stories you have read of Ambrose of Milan and John Chrysostom. Ambrose would not allow the Emperor any special place in the Church for that was the custom of the West. But in the Church of the East the Emperor even chose Bishops, and had an important place in the Church. Can you say which you think is the better custom, and why? What can we learn from the example of our own Queen?

7. Imagine that John Chrysostom came to your town and preached there. What kind of things do you think he would say? What things do you think he would criticise?

8. John Chrysostom always spoke what he thought was right and never cared whether he hurt people or not. Do you think

this is a good thing? Should we criticise people even if it hurts them, or try to speak kindly?

9. Imagine you lived in Constantinople when John Chrysostom was Bishop. Describe what he was like, what he said and did, and what people thought about him.

10. Add to your story of John Chrysostom his last prayer.

★

10. Ninian, Apostle of Scotland

THE Roman legions first went to Britain in 55 B.C. under the great Julius Caesar. But it was not till nearly 100 years later that they really conquered the island and made it part of the Roman Empire. Even then they could not defeat the fierce tribes who lived in Scotland or, as the Romans called it, Caledonia. These wild men tattooed their bodies so the Romans called them 'Picts' from the Roman word for 'painted'. When the Roman legions marched against them they hid in the hills. Then, when the Romans went back, they came down into the lowlands again to plunder. In A.D. 81 the Romans built a line of forts across Caledonia to keep the Picts out. It ran from the Firth of Clyde to the Firth of Forth. Later, a rampart of earth piled on stones was made along this line of forts and it was known as the Wall of Antonine.

Even this did not stop the Picts. In A.D. 121 the Emperor Hadrian had a new line of fortifications built further south. It ran from the Solway Firth to the mouth of the River Tyne and later on it was made even stronger. This is called Hadrian's Wall and its ruins can still be seen today. It was made of stone 5 metres high and was 116 kilometres in length. This great wall was guarded by thousands of soldiers who lived in its forts. So long as the Romans stayed in Britain to man it, Hadrian's wall did keep out the fierce and savage Picts.

In the year A.D. 360 a son was born to a chief who lived in Britain near Hadrian's Wall. He had become a Christian so his son was baptised and given the name of Ninian. When Ninian showed a great love for God, his father was glad and sent him to Rome so that he could have a good education. The Roman Emperors were Christian by that time and of course the wonderful Roman roads made travel easy. We can imagine how excited Ninian was to journey south, over the Channel and through Gaul, till he came to the greatest city in the world. At Rome there would be many things to interest him. But Ninian had one thought in his mind. Often as a boy he had heard stories of the savage Picts. Now he recognised that God was calling him to take the Good News of Jesus to them. So he studied hard in Rome to become a priest. In A.D. 394 he was made a bishop at Rome and set off to begin his great work for God.

Ninian sailed from Rome and landed in southern Gaul. On his journey northwards he stopped at Tours where the great St. Martin had his monastery. Ninian had heard of his fame and longed to meet him. They became great friends. Ninian saw how Martin trained his monks to go out in bands of twelve with a leader to

start a new monastery. Each monastery became a Christian outpost, for from it the monks went out to teach pagans the Gospel of Jesus. Every monk was a missionary. Ninian thought this was a wonderful way for Christians to convert the heathen. He decided that he would copy Martin in his work among the Picts.

It was in the year A.D. 397 that Ninian crossed over Hadrian's Wall and settled in the lowlands of Scotland. He made his way to the south-west and there he lived in a cave which can still be seen today. He began first to build his church. One ancient writer says that Martin had sent some monks to accompany Ninian. They were masons to help him build. The natives of Britain lived in crude huts built of wood and wattle. Ninian wanted a fine church that would be strong and beautiful. It was made of white stones and so it was called 'The White House' or, in the Roman language, 'Candida Casa'. Later on, the Saxons came to Britain and in their language 'White House' was 'Whit hern'. So the town which grew up there came to be called Whithorn and you can find it on your map of Scotland in Wigtownshire.

When his church was finished, Ninian and his monks built their monastery around it. Here they lived together devoting their time to worship and study. Ninian trained his monks just as Martin had done so that they could go out as missionaries among the Picts. He never forgot Martin and when he heard of the saint's death, he gave his 'White House' a new name—St. Martin's Church. Like Martin, too, he loved to be alone with

God. Often he went out to his cave in the cliffs, five kilometres away, just as Martin had done in his cave by the River Loire.

Soon the first monks were ready to go out and set up new monasteries among the Picts. Each one had its church and school for worship and study. Over the years these missions spread out over Scotland. But Ninian himself was not content to stay at the 'White House'. He led the way, going ever further North. It needed great courage to go alone and unarmed among the wild Picts, but Ninian never thought of himself. His goodness and love made him many friends and prepared the way for his monks. He worked among the Picts for thirty-five years till his death in A.D. 432. By then there were monasteries right up to the North and even across the sea in the Orkney and Shetland Islands.

So the 'White House' became the headquarters of a great missionary movement. Monks went out from it to the Picts in eastern Scotland; to the Scots in western Scotland and Ireland; to the Britons in England and in Wales. All this came from the work of Ninian and his name was revered far and wide. His body was buried in his own church and pilgrims came to Candida Casa to honour his memory. September 16th was set aside as his feast day so that Christians might never forget him. Later, Saint Columba came from Ireland and set up his monastery on the Island of Iona. His monks carried on the work of Ninian among the Picts, following in the footsteps of the great 'Apostle of Scotland'.

Questions and Things To Do

1. Find and read these passages in your Bible which remind us of Ninian—

The commandment of Jesus	St. Matthew 28. vv. 19–20
Witnesses of Jesus	Acts 1. v. 8
The call to a strange land	Acts 16. vv. 9–10.

2. Write your own account of the life of Ninian either in your notebook or in a special booklet.

3. Make your own map of Britain to show the places mentioned in this story. Draw arrows on your map to show how the monks of Ninian spread out on their missionary journeys.

4. Look back to the story of Martin of Tours and read it again. In what ways were Martin and Ninian alike? What did Ninian learn from Martin?

5. The natives of Britain made their homes of wattle, that is, by interlacing twigs, just as wicker baskets are made today. Many of Ninian's monastery buildings would be made in this way, too. Make a model of a monastery, showing the various buildings it would have grouped around the church.

6. Imagine you were a monk at Ninian's monastery at Candida Casa. Write or give an account of your life there and of what you thought of Ninian.

7. Ninian often went out to be alone in his cave, just as Jesus did. Why do we need sometimes to be alone with God? How does it help us in speaking with Him?

8. Find the hymns for saints in your hymn-book. Choose the one which you think would be best for Ninian. Read it together in choral speaking and learn it for use in school assembly.

9. Why do you think Ninian wanted to have a school at each of his monasteries? Why do you think monks were always so interested in education?

10. Make up a service for St. Ninian's Day. Choose a lesson you think suitable, hymns for the saint, and prayers. It would be very good to make up your own prayers, thanking God for the life and work of Ninian.

★

11. Gregory the Great

GREGORY was born in Rome in the year A.D. 540. His father was a ruler of the city for his family was rich and noble. Gregory had a happy and comfortable home and a good education. He studied law and when he was a man he, too, shared in the government of Rome. In A.D. 573 he was made the chief magistrate and had to judge between the citizens. He could be stern in seeing that justice was done but he won the love of many by his fairness and kindness. When his father died, soon after, he inherited great wealth and he could have lived in idleness and pleasure. But he was a sincere Christian and he wanted to serve his Master with all his heart. There were some monks in Rome who lived together by the Rule of the great St. Benedict. Gregory gave away all his wealth to the poor and joined them. Their simple life seemed to him very close to the life of Jesus and he followed it for the rest of his days.

When he was trained as a monk Gregory set up his own monastery in Rome named after St. Andrew, as well as six other monasteries on the island of Sicily. He lived happily at St. Andrew's, spending his time in prayer and study. But it was not long before the Bishop of Rome asked Gregory to help him in governing the Church. Gregory was sent to the great city of Constantinople, far away to the East. When he came back he was happy to enter his monastery again where he was made Abbot.

One day Abbot Gregory was going through the market-place where the merchants from near and far were selling their wares. One of them had some boys for sale as slaves. They had pleasant faces, fair hair and golden bodies, quite unlike the olive-skinned boys of Italy. Gregory stopped to admire them and asked where they came from. "They are pagans from Britain," replied the merchant. Gregory looked sad. "What are they called?" "Angles," answered the merchant. "Angles?" said Gregory. "They are indeed like angels. What part of the country do they come from?" "Deira," was the reply. "Good!" said the Abbot. "They must indeed be saved from 'Dei ira', the wrath of God, and brought to know their Saviour Christ. And who is their king?" "Aella," said the merchant. "Then Alleluia shall be sung to God in their land!" vowed Gregory.

He never forgot his promise. He longed to go to the land of the Angles and win them for Christ. As soon as he could, he set off on the long journey. But within three days messengers came from Rome and hustled him back. The Bishop had died from the plague and everyone wanted Gregory as their new Bishop. He gave in and accepted the great honour. But he never changed in any way during the fourteen years he was Bishop of Rome. Always he wore the simple rough garment or 'habit' of the monk. He chose for himself the title 'Servant of the servants of God'. For though he was the greatest man in Italy, Gregory was also the humblest.

He was a great leader both of the church and of his country. The Emperor lived far away in the East and had no real power in Italy. The fierce Lombards had invaded the land. There was fighting and lawlessness, plague and famine. By this time the Bishop of Rome owned large estates in the south of Italy and all the money from them. For emperors and rich men had given them over the years to the Church. Gregory used all this wealth for the good of the Church and people. He made a treaty with the Lombard invaders. He appointed governors for the cities. He provided for the sick and the poor. He was the ruler of Italy.

Gregory's influence spread all over Europe. By this time the Bishop of Rome, or the 'Pope' as he was known, had great power in the Church. Pope Gregory was greater than all those before him. He chose certain bishops in France and Spain and North Africa to be

his 'vicars', that is, his deputies. They acted for him and through them he ruled over the Church of the West.

Gregory never forgot the slave boys in the marketplace. If he could not be a missionary himself then he would send others. He chose a certain Augustine, the Prior of his own monastery at Rome. Augustine set off with forty monks on the long and adventurous journey.

78

While they were travelling through Gaul they heard dreadful stories of the cruel Angles and became frightened. The monks sent Augustine back to ask if they could return to Rome. Gregory gave him new hope and encouraged him to go on. So at last in A.D. 597 Augustine and his monks landed at Ebbsfleet in Kent and soon they had made a monastery at Canterbury. Gregory sent Augustine many letters, telling him what to do and giving him wise advice. So it was through this great Pope that Canterbury became the mother of the English Church.

Gregory never lost his love of learning and he wrote many books. One of them was a book to guide bishops in their work as shepherds of the flock of Christ. Later, King Alfred the Great translated it into the language of his people and Gregory's book was used by bishops for many centuries to come.

Gregory loved music best of all. He founded a 'School for Singers' in Rome. It was the very first 'Choir School' and through it the music of the church services became far more worthy. Gregory invented a new kind of singing for the services. It is called 'plain-song' or the 'Gregorian chant'. Though it was much simpler to sing, it was very beautiful and it was used in the monasteries where it is still sung today.

Gregory died in A.D. 604 and was at once made a saint of the Church. March 12th was set aside as his memorial day each year. On that day Christians remember his work as Bishop and Pope, missionary and musician, and thank God for the life of Gregory the Great.

Questions and Things To Do

1. Find and read in your Bible these passages which remind us of Gregory—

Poverty	St. Mark 10. v. 21
Humility	St. Matthew 18. v. 4
Servant of all	St. Mark 10. vv. 43–45
Singing to the Lord	Ephesians 5. v. 19.

2. Write your own story of the life of Gregory the Great. You could illustrate it with your own drawings of Gregory and his work.

A MORNING HYMN OF ST. GREGORY

Father, we praise Thee, now the night is over,
Active and watchful, stand we all before Thee;
Singing we offer praise and meditation:
Thus we adore Thee.

Monarch of all things, fit us for Thy mansions;
Banish our weakness, health and wholeness sending:
Bring us to heaven, where Thy saints united
Joy without ending.

All-holy Father, Son and equal Spirit,
Trinity blessed, send us Thy salvation;
Thine is the glory, gleaming and resounding
Through all creation.

3. Write out the 'Morning Hymn' of Gregory and add it to your account. Read it together in choral speaking and learn it to use in school assembly. You could also use it as a prayer.

4. We learn much about Gregory from the first English history book. It was written by a monk named Bede and it is called 'A History of the English Church and People'. There is a fine translation of it in the Penguin Classics series. Find a copy of this book and see what Bede says about Gregory in Book 2 Chapter 1. You will find many interesting stories in it besides the story of the slave boys.

5. Use reference books to find out more about 'plain-song' singing. Some of our hymn tunes come from it. See if you can find any in your hymn-book. The monks used to write the service books in their beautiful 'illuminated' writing, both music and words. (See page 79.) Write out one of your favourite hymns in this way.

6. When Gregory made a bishop in another land his 'vicar' or 'deputy', he gave him a 'pall'. The Roman word 'pallium' means a cloak. The pall was his badge as a senior bishop. It was made of lamb's wool in a nunnery at Rome. It was shaped like a circle and hung back and front over the shoulders. It was pure white and had four crosses marked on it. Draw or paint the coat of arms of the Archbishop of Canterbury which shows exactly what a pall was like.

7. The Bishop of Rome is called the Pope. This word comes from the Greek word 'pappas' which is the childish form of 'pater', meaning 'father'. Still today a priest in the Church of the East is called 'Papas' by his people. In the West it was a title for any bishop. But in 1073 the Bishop of Rome said it must not be used for any other bishop. The Pope is the head of the Roman Catholic Church. Write this meaning in your note-book.

8. Monks live by three rules—poverty, chastity and obedience. Why do you think monks have these three vows?

9. Find out all you can about Augustine's mission to England and write an account of it with your own illustrations.

10. Find out all you can about Canterbury and write your own history of it.

★

12. Paulinus of York

In the year A.D. 410 the Roman Emperor ordered the Roman legions to leave Britain. Savage tribes were attacking the borders of the Empire; Italy had been invaded and the great city of Rome was threatened. Every soldier was needed and Britain had to be given up. Even the Romans had never been able to conquer the fierce Picts who lived in Scotland or the savage Scots who came from Ireland. Now new enemies faced the Britons. Jutes, Saxons and Angles came in their pirate ships from Europe. The Britons were driven back to the west of the island and the invaders ruled the land. Britain was divided up into seven kingdoms under the Anglo-Saxons who were the forefathers of the English race.

The kingdom of Kent was ruled over by the great King Ethelbert when Augustine landed there in A.D. 597 Augustine and his forty monks had been sent by Pope Gregory from his own monastery at Rome. Gregory had never forgotten the fair-haired boys he had seen in the slave-market at Rome. He longed to go to Britain himself but when he became Pope he could not leave Rome. Augustine and his monks were frightened by the stories they heard of the wild pagans in England but Gregory urged them on. When they landed in Kent, things went well for them at first. King Ethelbert had married a lady named Bertha, daughter of the King of Paris who ruled over the Franks. She was a Christian and she persuaded her husband to receive the monks and to listen to them.

ANGLO-SAXON
KINGDOMS
IN THE TIME OF
PAULINUS

WHITBY
YORK
LINCOLN
NORTHUMBRIA
MERCIA
EAST ANGLIA
ESSEX
LONDON
ROCHESTER
CANTERBURY
WESSEX
SUSSEX
KENT

NORTHUMBRIA WAS MADE OUT OF TWO
EARLIER KINGDOMS—DEIRA AND BERNICIA
LAND HELD BY THE BRITONS

Ethelbert gave them freedom to preach to his people. Queen Bertha used the old Roman church of St. Martin's at Canterbury. This became their church until they had built their monastery. Ethelbert himself became a Christian and the Church grew.

Pope Gregory was very anxious to help Augustine in his work. He wrote long letters giving him wise advice. Then four years later, he sent Augustine his pall, his badge of office as Archbishop. It was brought by four priests, whom Gregory sent to help Augustine, together with a letter. It was addressed to "our most holy brother Augustine from Gregory, servant of the servants of God". In it Gregory told Augustine to make twelve more bishops in southern England, especially one for London. He must also send a bishop to York, a city founded by the Romans, who would have twelve bishops under him in the north of England.

One of the four priests sent by Gregory was named Paulinus. He was a wise leader and a fine preacher, and he became the first Archbishop of York. In A.D. 625 King Ethelbert's daughter married Edwin the King of Northumbria, and Paulinus went with her to her new home. Her name was Ethelberga and she was a Christian like her parents. King Edwin believed in the pagan gods but he promised that Ethelberga could bring a bishop with her and worship her own God freely. King Edwin was a serious man and he often wondered whether to give up his gods. He decided to call a meeting of all his nobles and they gathered in the King's great hall. Edwin asked each of them what they thought. The chief of the heathen priests was honest. He said their gods did not seem very powerful. Then one of the nobles spoke thus. "It seems to me, O King, that man is like a sparrow

which darts into this hall in the winter when we are feasting. It comes out of the dark night through the open doorway. It flutters for a time in the light and warmth. Then it flies out through the doorway at the other end into the darkness. The life of man is like that. He comes into this world from we know not where. He lives on earth for a short time in the light and warmth. Then he goes out into the darkness we call death. Can this new religion tell us where he comes from, why he is here on earth and where he goes after he dies? If it can, we should give up our gods and worship the God of Paulinus." Then Paulinus spoke and showed how the Christian religion answered all these questions. The King and the nobles heard him gladly. The idols were broken down by the chief priest himself. King Edwin was baptised at York on Easter Day in the year 627 A.D. and his chieftains followed him into the Christian Church.

For six years Paulinus was Bishop of York. He travelled throughout the kingdom of Northumbria, preaching and teaching and baptising in the flowing rivers. In his history book the monk Bede says that often from dawn to dusk he did nothing but proclaim the Good News of Jesus. He describes Paulinus as a tall man, stooping a little, with dark hair and a thin face. His wonderful work made the people of Northumbria peaceful and banished evil. It was said that a mother could carry her baby from coast to coast across the land and come to no harm.

In A.D. 633 the Pope sent the pall to Paulinus, making him Archbishop of York. A cathedral was begun in the city as well as many other churches throughout the king-

dom. Paulinus travelled as far south as the city of Lincoln where he built a fine stone church. It was there that he gave the pall to the new Archbishop of Canterbury on behalf of the Pope. But that very same year the good King Edwin was attacked by Penda, the heathen King of Mercia, and killed in battle. The pagans roamed through Northumbria, killing and looting. Paulinus made his way to the coast with Queen Ethelberga and took her by ship to safety in her own kingdom of Kent. He carried with him a gold cross and a gold cup from his church at York and placed them in the cathedral church of Canterbury.

Paulinus could not go back to York where the heathens were doing all they could to wipe out Christianity. Instead he became Bishop of Rochester in the kingdom of

Kent. There he laboured for eleven years till his death in A.D. 644. We shall see in our next story that his work in Northumbria had not been in vain. He will always be remembered as the first Archbishop of York, especially on October 10th, the day set aside to the memory of this great saint of the Church.

Questions and Things To Do

1. Find and read in your Bible these passages which remind us of Paulinus—

The work of the missionary	St. Matthew 28. v. 19
The Good News in Jesus	Romans 5. v. 8.
Preaching the Gospel	1 Corinthians 15. vv. 1–4
The church of God	Ephesians 4. vv. 4–6.

2. Make your own map of England to illustrate the life of Paulinus. Show on it the Anglo-Saxon Kingdoms and the places mentioned in this story. Fix it in your notebook.

3. The boats of the Anglo-Saxon pirates had flat bottoms. They were twenty-two metres long and about two metres wide. They were made of oak beams tied with ropes made of bark and with bolts of iron. A boat contained fifty warriors, each rowing with his oar when necessary. For weapons they had axes, swords and knives. You can find a list of their chief gods on page 32. Imagine you lived in England in those days. Describe the invaders who came to pillage your land. Reference books will help you to find out more about them.

4. You can find many stories of England at this period in our first history book, 'A History of the English Church and People', written by the Venerable Bede. Borrow this book and read it as you have time. The story of Paulinus is told in Book 2, chapters 9, 12–14, 16–18 and 20.

5. King Edwin's nobleman said that there are three great questions—Where do we come from? Why are we in this world? Where do we go after death? How do you think Paulinus answered these three questions? What would he have said?

6. Paulinus baptised mostly adult people, for they had never heard of Jesus before. He baptised them in rivers. We are used to children being baptised in our churches at the font. Find out what happens in your own church at a baptism, and write or give an account of it. Draw or model the kind of font used in your church.

7. Paulinus taught the Christian faith to a princess named Hilda and baptised her. When she grew up, she became the Abbess of the famous monastery at Whitby where Caedmon the cowherd sang the praises of God. You can read about Hilda and Caedmon in another book in this series, 'Heroes of the Faith'. Find out all you can about Hilda and write an account of life at her monastery.

8. Use reference books to find out all you can about the city of York and to make a short history of it.

9. The cup which Paulinus took to Canterbury is called a chalice. Find out the meaning of this word and what such a cup is used for in church.

10. Can you remember what a 'pall' is? Describe and design one.

★

13. Oswald, the Martyr King

NORTHUMBRIA was a happy place to live in during the reign of good King Edwin. He joined together the two small kingdoms of Deira and Bernicia and made his new kingdom the greatest in the whole of England. Queen Ethelberga had come from Kent bringing with her the Christian bishop Paulinus. He was the first Archbishop of York, the capital city of Northumbria, and in A.D. 627 Edwin himself had become a Christian. Through the work of Paulinus, Northumbria became a peaceful and happy kingdom. But other kings were jealous of Edwin. In A.D. 633 Penda, the heathen King of Mercia, rose against Edwin. He found an ally in Cadwallon, King of Wales, and they joined their armies together. Edwin had to go out to meet them and in a fierce battle near Doncaster he was slain. Cadwallon and his savage soldiers went through the land with fire and sword. Northumbria became two separate kingdoms again.

Deira became pagan once more, and Cadwallon ruled over it with great cruelty. But the men of Bernicia would not surrender. They had an excellent leader in Oswald, a royal prince who came back to win his kingdom. When Oswald's father had been killed in battle, he and his two brothers had been taken to safety. They had been brought up on an island called Iona, off the west coast of Scotland. Fifty years before, a monk from Ireland, named

Columba, had settled there. On it was a fine monastery with a church and school, bake-house and dairy, cows and sheep. Oswald's father had been a pagan but at Iona Oswald and his brothers grew up as Christians. Then the news came that Edwin had been slain and his kingdom was being harried by

England in the time of
KING OSWALD

Kingdoms are underlined

the heathen. At once Oswald and his brothers set off back to their own country. His elder brother was killed by the treachery of Cadwallon so Oswald became the rightful king. The brave men of Bernicia rallied to him but Oswald's army was small compared with the huge host of Cadwallon. Before the battle Oswald ordered his men to make a big wooden cross. It was set up in the ground for all to see. Then he bade his men kneel down while he led them in prayer. They rose up, strong in their faith, and advanced against their enemies. The battle was fierce and long but at last Cadwallon was slain and his army fled. Ever afterwards the battlefield was known as 'Heaven's Field' and a

91

church was built there. It lay near the town of Hexham, close to the great Roman wall.

Once more King Oswald joined together Deira and Bernicia to make his kingdom of Northumbria. He ruled over it for seven years and showed himself a good and great king. One of his very first acts was to send an urgent message to the monks at Iona. "Come to Northumbria," he begged. "Come and teach my people the true faith so that they may give up their pagan gods and live in peace and goodness." The monks chose Aidan, a holy and gentle man of God, and he came to the king's fortress at Bamborough near the east coast of Northumberland. At first Aidan could not speak the language of the people. But King Oswald taught him and soon he could go about among the people alone. "Where would you like to build your monastery?" the King asked. "I

come from Iona, an island," said Aidan. "I should like to live on your island of Lindisfarne." So Aidan built his monastery there and lived with his monks. It was easy to walk across to the mainland when the tide was low. Aidan and his monks travelled through the land, preaching and teaching, building churches and schools. Aidan became greatly loved. He travelled everywhere on foot, a friend to everyone he met. Many of the heathens became Christians and many churches were built. King Oswald helped him in every way he could. His own example helped most of all and many of his chieftains were baptised. Lindisfarne became famous for its great monastery and still today it bears the lovely name it earned under Aidan—Holy Island.

The monk Bede tells us in his history book how happy the kingdom of Northumbria was under King Oswald. Aidan and his monks spread the Good News of the Gospel throughout the land. The King gave both money and lands for the building of new monasteries. He completed the fine church at York which Paulinus had started. Both rich and poor, nobles and peasants, were taught the Christian faith. Soon many were living as Christians in peace and goodwill with one another. Oswald became a great King for he ruled over Britons and Picts and Scots as well as his own Anglo-Saxon people. Yet he was always humble and generous. Bede tells how one Easter he sat down with Bishop Aidan to a great feast when a servant came in. He told the King that a crowd of beggars waited outside. At once the King ordered the

servant to take out to them his own food as well as the silver dish which lay before him.

It was through the good influence of Oswald that other kingdoms were won to the Church. In A.D. 635 the King of Wessex was baptised in the presence of Oswald, who gladly became his godfather and gave him his daughter in marriage. But Penda, the heathen King of Mercia, still hated him and only waited for a chance to attack Oswald. At last he was ready and he invaded Northumbria. Penda believed fiercely in his pagan gods and was determined to wipe out the Christian religion which he hated so much. The armies met at the battle of Maserfield in A.D. 642 and Oswald was slain, his body covered with arrows. His head was cut off by Penda. Bishop Aidan buried it reverently. Many years later it was found and placed in the cathedral at Durham, where it lies to this day.

Penda was finally defeated and killed by Oswald's younger brother who became King after him. Oswald had given his life for his faith in God. The Church set aside August 5th as the day sacred to the memory of this martyr King.

Questions and Things To Do

1. Find and read in your Bible these passages which remind us of Oswald—

A wise king	1 Kings 3. vv. 11–14
A king builds a church	1 Kings 6. vv. 11–14
A king's prayer	1 Kings 8. vv. 22–24, 27–30.

2. Imagine you were the boy Oswald being brought up by the monks at Iona. Write a letter, say to a friend in York, to describe your life there. Reference books will help you to find out more about Columba's monastery and about monastic life in those days.

3. You can read about both Columba and Aidan in 'Heroes of the Faith'. Find out all you can about them and write a short history of both these saints.

4. King Oswald reminds us in many ways of King Alfred the Great, whom you can also read about in 'Heroes of the Faith'. Can you think of ways in which they were alike and ways in which their lives were similar to each other?

5. Make your own map of England in the time of King Oswald. Mark on it the kingdoms and places mentioned in this story. Be sure to include the islands of Iona and Lindisfarne.

6. What do we mean by the word 'martyr'? The first Christian martyr was Stephen, whom you can read about in Acts 6. v. 8 and 7 vv. 54–60. How many other Christian martyrs can you name and describe?

7. Deira was the kingdom from which the slave boys came whom Pope Gregory saw in the market-place at Rome. Can you remember what Latin words Deira reminded Gregory of and what they mean? You can read this story on page 77.

8. You can read stories of King Oswald in 'A History of the English Church and People' by the monk Bede. You can find them in Book 3, chapters 1–3, 6–7 and 9–14.

9. In what ways do you think a king or queen can help their people to live as Christians? How did Oswald help his people? What can we learn from the example of our own Queen?

10. Imagine you were a page-boy or a servant girl in the fortress at Bamborough where King Oswald lived. Describe what he was like, how he lived, and how he ruled over his people. You can describe, too, Bishop Aidan who often came to the king's rooms to talk with him about his work.

★

14. Chad and Cedd, the Brother Bishops

WHEN Oswald became King of Northumbria he wanted most of all to bring his heathen people to know the true God. He asked the monks on the island of Iona, where he had been brought up, to come and help him. They sent a party led by Aidan, a holy and gentle man of God.

Aidan set up his monastery on another island called
Lindisfarne, off the east coast of Northumbria. There
the monks made their home. Their chief buildings were
the church and the school. For, if their work was to go
on, they must train boys who would carry on after them,
preaching and teaching the Good News of Jesus. The
school at Lindisfarne became very famous and important,
for many of its boys grew up to become bishops and monks.

Among the boys at Aidan's school were four who were
all brothers. When they grew up, all of them became
priests. Two of them, Cedd and Chad, became bishops
and saints of the church. Cedd, the eldest of the brothers,
began his great work in Mercia where Penda the pagan
was King. Penda hated Christianity but his children did
not. For his daughter married the son of Oswy, King of

England in the time of
CEDD AND CHAD

NORTHUMBRIA

Lindisfarne Island

Whitby

York

Lichfield

MERCIA

ESSEX Bradwell-on-Sea.
Tilbury

Canterbury

Northumbria. Oswy had become King when his brother Oswald was killed in battle. He, too, was a Christian and had brought his children up to love the true God. When Penda's son wanted to marry the daughter of Oswy, Oswy refused unless he became a Christian. He was a fine young man and when he had been taught the Christian faith he was gladly baptised. He went back home with his bride, taking four Christian priests with him. One of them was Cedd. So Christianity came to heathen Mercia.

But Cedd's great work was to be done among the East Saxons in their kingdom of Essex. Their King named Sigbert was a great friend of King Oswy and often went to visit him in Northumbria. Oswy was always telling him how silly it was to make gods out of logs or blocks of stone and to worship them. At last Sigbert was won to the true God and was baptised on one of his visits to Oswy. He asked Oswy for Christian teachers to instruct his people and Cedd gladly went back with him. He was a good missionary and in A.D. 654 he was made Bishop of the East Saxons. He trained priests to help him in his work and built churches. He set up new monasteries at Tilbury and at Bradwell-on-Sea and from them the monks went far and wide preaching the Gospel.

Sometimes Cedd went back to Northumbria. One of his brothers was chaplain to the King of Dcira and through him the King came to know the holy Cedd. He asked Cedd to found a monastery where he might go to pray and to hear the word of God. Cedd gladly agreed and he chose a lonely place in the hills called Lastingham, near the town of Whitby. There he taught the monks to live just as he had lived at Lindisfarne as a boy, and he himself was the first Abbot.

In the year A.D. 664 a great meeting of lcaders of the Church was arranged. It was held at the famous monastery at Whitby, ruled over by the Abbess Hilda. Bishop Cedd was asked to go and he acted as leader, for everyone knew that he would be fair and just. When the meeting was over he went back to his monastery at Lastingham. It was a time of plague and we can be sure that Bishop Cedd helped to nurse the sick monks. Soon he himself caught the disease and died, as he would have wished, in his own monastery.

Cedd ordered that his brother Chad should become Abbot of Lastingham after him. But the next year King Oswy sent for him to become Bishop of his people at York, for Wilfrid, the former Bishop, had gone abroad and Oswy needed a man of God in his city. Chad was a holy

man and humble in spite of his great learning. He refused to ride on horseback and went about on foot like the Apostles of Jesus. The people met their Bishop in the towns and in the countryside. He was at home in both cottage and castle, friend of all. But when Bishop Wilfrid came back from abroad in A.D. 669, Chad humbly gave place to him and went back to his monastery at Lastingham.

But in the very same year the holy Chad was called out of his monastery again. Penda, the heathen king of Mercia, had been killed in battle with Oswy, and his son Wulfhere reigned in his place. Wulfhere had become a Christian and he asked for a bishop. Chad was sent to Mercia by Theodore the Archbishop of Canterbury. He still loved to travel on foot but he was getting old and Theodore ordered him to ride a horse on his journeys.

The holy Chad still thought he should walk like Jesus and His apostles. So Theodore brought a horse and he himself helped Chad to mount it!

Chad set up his bishopric at Lichfield. He built a little house near the church where he and his monks could live and pray and study together. But it was not often he could stay there as he loved to do. For he travelled far and wide through the great kingdom of Mercia preaching the Gospel of love. Often he came back to his house, worn out by his travels. It was there that he died on March 2nd in the year A.D. 672.

One of Chad's own monks taught the Venerable Bede from whose history book we learn all these things. He told Bede stories of the saint, of his humility and love to both men and God. If a storm arose while he was studying, he would kneel and pray for God's mercy on all mankind or go to his church to say prayers and psalms. He lived a simple life, taking little food and sleep, refusing to have any possessions. His whole life was spent in the service of God and his holiness won many pagans to Him.

Cedd is remembered on January 7th in the Christian year and Chad on March 2nd. For both were made saints of the Church so that men might never forget the missionary zeal and the holy example of these brother bishops.

Questions and Things To Do

1. Find and read these passages in your Bible which remind us of Cedd and Chad—

Learning about God at school Deuteronomy 6. vv. 4–7
Preaching the Gospel   St. Mark 16. v. 15
Workers for God   St. Luke 9. vv. 1–6

2. Both Cedd and Chad were brought up in a monastery and both were monks and Abbots. The word 'Abbot' comes from the word 'Abba' which meant 'Father' in the language Jesus spoke (see St. Mark 14. v. 36). Find out all you can about a monastery and its buildings and make a model of one. See if you can find the proper names for each part of it.

3. Make your own map of England as it was in the time of Cedd and Chad and mark on it all the places mentioned in this story.

4. Both Cedd and Chad were very humble men. What do we mean by 'humility'? What can we learn from Jesus about being humble? What can we learn from Chad?

5. Both Cedd and Chad were missionaries. How would you describe a missionary? What is his work? What modern missionaries can you name?

6. Why do you think Chad always went about on foot rather than on horseback? Do you think this was sensible? What can we learn from his reasons for doing this?

7. Both Cedd and Chad became bishops. Find out all you can about a bishop's life and work, what he wears and carries in church, and what these things stand for. If you have bishops in your church find out about your own bishop. Write an account of what you find and add to it a drawing of a bishop in his special robes.

8. Find the nearest monastery or ruin of a monastery to where you live and visit it if you can. Make your own short 'history' of it. It would be very good if you could write the history of one of the monasteries mentioned in this story.

9. Find the hymns for saints in your hymn-book and choose one for Cedd and one for Chad, saying why you chose it. Read through the hymns you choose in choral speaking and learn them for school assembly.

10. Make up a service for Cedd or Chad, selecting a lesson, hymns and prayers. It would be very good to make up your own prayers.

★

15. Wilfrid, the Apostle of Sussex

WILFRID was born in the kingdom of Northumbria in the year A.D. 634 His father was a chieftain and when he took his son to court the Queen liked the handsome and clever boy. Wilfrid was fourteen years old then but he had already made up his mind to be a monk. The Queen asked the monks of Lindisfarne to take Wilfrid into their school. He was a studious boy, always learning, and the monks liked him, too, for his humility and obedience. When he was twenty years old Wilfrid decided to visit Rome. The Pope of Rome was the most important bishop in the Church and Wilfrid wanted to study the ways of the Church there. The Queen gladly agreed and she gave him a letter to the King of Kent, asking him to help Wilfrid on his journey. Wilfrid stayed for a time at

The
Life of
WILFRID

Lindisfarne Island

NORTHUMBRIA

Whitby

Ripon
York

SOUTH
SAXONS
Canterbury
Chichester
Selsey

FRISIANS

Paris

Canterbury, learning the customs of the Church there. Then he crossed over to France. The Bishop of the city of Lyons was specially kind to Wilfrid and he too helped him with money and a guide for his journey.

When he came to Rome, Wilfrid studied eagerly the ways of the Church there. He found they were different from the customs of the Church in Northumbria. The monks there lived by the Rule of Benedict which Wilfrid thought much better than the life of the monks at Lindisfarne. He found, too, that the Church at Rome kept Easter at a different time from his own church in England. There were many other differences and Wilfrid was sure that the church at Rome was right. It had been founded by the Apostle Peter, whereas the monks in England had worked out their own customs. Wilfrid determined to bring the customs of Rome to England. He studied hard in Rome and on his way back home stayed again at Lyons where the bishop gladly made him a monk.

The King of Northumbria welcomed Wilfrid back by giving him a monastery with much land at a place called Ripon. The monks there would not accept the new Roman Customs and they went back to their old monastery. Wilfrid made his new monks live by the Rule of Benedict. He became their Abbot in A.D. 661. But he was not left long to rule his monastery. The King of Northumbria needed this clever and learned man to advise him. A great meeting of church leaders was held in A.D. 664 at the monastery of Whitby where the Abbess Hilda ruled. It was to decide whether the Church in England should follow its own ways or the customs of the Church of Rome which were obeyed everywhere else in Europe. Wilfrid was a splendid speaker. He described the Roman customs and urged everyone to follow the Apostle Peter and not their own ways. The council agreed to do this and the King asked Wilfrid to become the Bishop of Northumbria. Wilfrid went to Paris where he would be made a bishop according to the Roman customs. But he stayed there so long that the King made the holy Chad bishop in his place. When at last Wilfrid came back, the humble Chad returned to his monastery and Wilfrid became Bishop of York in A.D. 669. For nearly ten years he worked there, travelling through the land preaching the Gospel and building churches. He finished the wonderful Minster Church at York which had been first started by Bishop Paulinus over thirty years before. He showed his priests how to sing the services as they did in Rome and to make them more worthy of the worship of God.

Wilfrid was a fine leader but he was obstinate too.

He quarrelled with the Archbishop of Canterbury and decided to go to Rome to appeal to the Pope. On the way his ship was driven ashore in Holland where the wild Frisians lived. Wilfrid fearlessly preached to them and to their King and won them to worship the true God. He was the first Christian missionary to visit them and later others carried on the work he had begun. When the winter ended he went on to Rome. The Pope sided with Wilfrid in his quarrel with the Archbishop, but when he came back to England Wilfrid still could not get his own way. So he journeyed south to the land of the South Saxons, now called Sussex.

The people there were fair-haired and handsome. But they were pagans and savage in their ways. Wilfrid knew

106

what they were like, for some years before on a journey his ship had been driven on to their sandy coast and they had attacked it. Wilfrid and his companions had only escaped with their lives when the tide floated their vessel off the beach. He had never forgotten those childlike savages. So he planned to bring to them the Christian way of peace and friendship. He went among them without fear. Armed with their spears they crowded round him, puzzled by this strange man who carried no weapons. Wilfrid found them suffering from famine after a long drought. He taught them to catch fish in their wicker coracles and showed himself to be their friend. Thus he won their trust and soon he was able to speak to them of Jesus and His love. He built his little church at Selsey and through his brave toil the South Saxons were brought into the fold of the Church of Christ.

After some years in Sussex Wilfrid was called back to his bishopric of York. He spent the last few years of his life peacefully in his monastery at Ripon where he died in 709 A.D. His monks buried him lovingly near the altar in the church he himself had built. The epitaph they wrote above his tomb told of his stormy life. He had made the dangerous journey to Rome three times in all, and often he had known the perils of the sea. He had risked his life among the wild men of Frisia and the savages of South Sussex. He had stood firmly for the customs of the Roman Church, facing quarrels and enmity for what he believed to be right. For 45 years he had been a faithful bishop of the Church. October 12th was set aside as his feast day so that men should never forget the brave Apostle of Sussex.

Questions and Things To Do

1. Find and read in your Bible these passages which remind us of Wilfrid—

The call of the missionary	St. Mark 16. v. 15
Facing dangers	2 Corinthians 11. vv. 26–28
The armour of God	Ephesians 6. vv. 14–18.

2. Make your own map of England in the time of Wilfrid, marking on it the places mentioned in this story of his life.

3. Wilfrid brought back to his monastery the Rule of St. Benedict. You can read about Benedict in another book in this series, 'The Church Marches On'. Benedict's Rule divided the

monk's day between work and study and prayer. Find out all you can about it and write an account of a Benedictine monastery, illustrating it with your own drawings.

4. Benedict said, "To work is to pray: to pray is to work." What do you think he meant by this? Why should he insist that his monks did work with their hands as well as study and prayer?

5. Coracles are still used today by some fishermen in the West country and in Wales. Make a model of a coracle, in wicker work if you can, or draw one. If you draw it you might like to show Wilfrid in your picture teaching the South Saxons to fish.

6. Wilfrid was so sure that he was right that he sometimes seems to have been an obstinate and quarrelsome man. Do you think we should risk quarrelling with other people in standing up for the right? Or should we say nothing in case we offend them?

7. Imagine you were a boy or girl of the South Saxons when Wilfrid first came to live among you. Describe what you think he was like, what he did, and what your people thought about him.

8. 'Minster' comes from an Anglo-Saxon word and means 'the church of a monastery'. Find out all you can about York Minster and write a short history of it, with illustrations if you can. Or you can do the same for the beautiful cathedral of Chichester which stands today as a memorial to Wilfrid's work in Sussex.

9. Make up a service for St. Wilfrid's Day. Choose a lesson and hymns which you think suitable. Choose prayers or, better still, make up a prayer of your own, thanking God for Wilfrid and his work.

10. Why do you think Wilfrid was such a brave man, going among savages? Read in your Bible Joshua 1. vv. 5–6. How do they help us to understand the courage of missionaries like Wilfrid?

★

16. Cuthbert of Lindisfarne

EVEN when he was a young boy Cuthbert, like Wilfrid, knew that he wanted to be a monk. He went to the monastery at Melrose, by the River Tweed, as a lad. The Abbot was a good and gentle man and Cuthbert himself grew in holiness. As soon as he was old enough he took the monk's vows of poverty, chastity and obedience. When the Prior of Melrose died, Cuthbert was chosen to fill his place. He trained the boys and young men there in the monastic life. He taught them with authority, but he taught them best by his own simple goodness.

Many monks stayed in the monastery all their lives. Cuthbert loved to go out and travel among the people in the towns and villages, preaching the Gospel of Jesus. Sometimes he rode on a horse but he mostly went on foot. The people of Northumbria had not long been Christians and they easily fell back into their pagan ways. This happened especially in time of plague. There were no doctors or hospitals, except in the monasteries. The simple folk tried to stop the plague by calling on the gods.

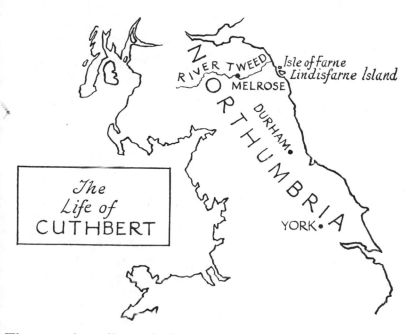

The Life of CUTHBERT

They used spells and charms and magic arts. Cuthbert went out into the countryside particularly at these times. He taught them to give up such foolish ways and to make their prayers to the one true God.

When Cuthbert came to a town, people quickly gathered together. They listened eagerly to his preaching and gladly tried to live as he taught them. There was something different from other monks about Cuthbert. When he spoke, his face shone like an angel. So great was his love that his hearers felt ashamed. They had to own up to him any wrong they had done. Nothing could be hidden from the saintly Prior. Then he gently told them how they should show God they were sorry.

Cuthbert did not often go to the towns. He loved best to go to the lonely villages tucked among the mountains, where the people never saw a stranger, for visitors feared to go there. The people were rough and poor and there were dangers on all sides. Sometimes Cuthbert was away in the mountains for a month at a time, teaching the lonely villagers the ways of God by his words and his example of love and kindness.

In the year A.D. 664 Cuthbert went with his Abbot to the monastery at Lindisfarne to be Prior there. His work was to train the monks and to teach the boys in the famous school of Lindisfarne. But after some years on the island, Cuthbert felt called by God to live alone. He loved his fellow monks but that was because he loved

God most of all. He longed to be alone with God. He chose another island nearby named the Isle of Farne. No one dared to live there for it was believed to be the abode of evil spirits. Nor was there any water or trees. First Cuthbert drove out the evil spirits in the name of God. Then the monks willingly came to help him build a little hut for his new home. He bade them dig for water where he directed and there they found a clear flowing spring. He sowed barley and his good crop gave him food to support himself. Round the hut Cuthbert built a high wall of earth so that he could see nothing but the heavens. For eight years he lived the life of a hermit on his tiny island of Farne.

The fame of the holy Cuthbert spread throughout the kingdom of Northumbria. In A.D. 685 a council of bishops elected him to be Bishop of Northumbria. Messengers were sent to the island to fetch Cuthbert but he would not come. Then the King himself, with leaders of the church and the monks of Lindisfarne, went by boat to the island. They knelt before the saint and pleaded with him to become their bishop. At last the humble Cuthbert gave in to their entreaties and on Easter Day he was made Bishop in the Minster at York.

Bishop Cuthbert lived like the Apostles of Jesus. He was simple in his ways, fasting and denying himself. He was always humble and saw no difference between high and low, rich and poor, noble and peasant. He spent much of his time in prayer for the people given to his charge. His teaching won them to love God and each other. He was, as Bede says in his history book, the

finest kind of teacher for he himself practised what he taught. His love and patience and kindness showed men what Jesus must have been like and they longed to be like him. He was never too busy to help anyone and he loved best to help those who had gone astray and needed him most. He was only a Bishop for two years. But during that time he did wonderful work for the Church in Northumbria.

Cuthbert was growing old and, when he knew the end of his life was near, he went back to his little island home to spend his last days with God. Some of the monks accompanied their beloved bishop. He wanted to be buried on the island he had loved best of all. But the monks pleaded with him to let them bury him on the

Holy Island of Lindisfarne, within their own church. Cuthbert died on March 20th in the year A.D. 687 and was buried at Lindisfarne. In the years to come the Danes invaded England and Lindisfarne knew no peace. When at last England was united and fighting ended, the body of Cuthbert was taken to the Cathedral at Durham where it rests to this day.

Some of the saints we have read about in this book served God as leaders of the Church, others as missionaries, and others as builders of churches. Cuthbert served God best of all by the simple goodness of his life. The day of his death, March 20th, was set aside in the Christian year as his festival day. On it Christians have always remembered him and given thanks to God for the holiness of his life and for the example he gives us of Christian love.

Questions and Things To Do

1. Find and read these passages in your Bible which remind us of Cuthbert—

    The Christian character   St. Matthew 5. vv. 1–12
    The two commandments of   St. Mark 12. vv. 30–31
      Jesus
    The badge of the Christian   St. John 13. v. 35
    The fruits of the Spirit   Galatians 5. v. 22.

2. Imagine you were a boy or girl in one of the mountain villages when Cuthbert came. Describe what he was like, what he did, and what people thought about the visitor.

3. Make your own map to illustrate the life of Cuthbert, marking on it the places mentioned in this story.

4. The Beatitudes in St. Matthew 5. vv. 1–12 seem to describe exactly the kind of person Cuthbert was. Read them together in choral speaking. That will help you to know them by heart as you should.

5. There are several incidents in this story of Cuthbert for you to draw. You can draw his life in a series of pictures as a strip cartoon.

6. You should know by heart the two commandments of Jesus in St. Mark 12. vv. 30–31. Why does Jesus put love for God first? How does loving God help us to love other people? Can we love other people without loving God?

7. Why do you think Cuthbert wanted to live alone as a hermit on the island of Farne?

8. Cuthbert was a Prior, not an Abbot. The Abbot ruled over the whole of the monastery. The Prior was the chief monk, and his work was to train and to teach the monks. Make a note of these meanings.

9. What do you think were the good things in the character of Cuthbert? Make a list of them and explain carefully what each of them means.

10. Make up a service for St. Cuthbert's Day. Choose carefully hymns which you think best describe the kind of person he was—hymns like 'Blest are the pure in heart'. Read them through in choral speaking and learn them to use in school assembly. Choose a lesson, perhaps one of those mentioned above. Choose suitable prayers or, better still, make up a prayer of your own.

★

17. Willibrord, Apostle of the Netherlands

YOU will remember that Wilfrid, the Apostle of Sussex, had been given the monastery of Ripon by the King of Northumbria. There he taught his monks to live by the Rule of Benedict which he had learnt on his journeys to Rome. There too he set up a school to train boys in the Christian faith. One day a new boy, named Willibrord, came to the school. He had been born in Northumbria in A.D. 659. His father had decided to become a hermit

The Life of WILLIBRORD

and he sent Willibrord to be brought up by the monks. He was not a great scholar but he grew up with a great love of God.

When he was twenty years old, Willibrord went across the sea to a monastery in Ireland. It was at Mellifont in County Louth. There he stayed for twelve years, during which he became a priest. A bishop lived nearby named Egbert, who had a great longing to preach the Good News of Jesus to the pagans who lived in Europe. He had set sail once himself but shipwreck had forced him to return home. Now he was too old to set out again. Willibrord listened to him eagerly and determined to go to the heathen. In the year A.D. 690 he set sail with twelve friends for Europe.

The little band of monks landed near the mouth of the River Rhine. Their aim was to work among the Frisians, a wild tribe who lived in Holland and Belgium. For when Willibrord had been at Ripon monastery he had heard Abbot Wilfrid talk about them. Wilfrid had once been shipwrecked on their coast and had spent a whole winter amongst them. They were a simple and savage people but he had found them willing to listen to the Good News of Jesus. No Christians had been to them since. Willibrord wanted to carry on the fine work begun by his old Abbot.

First he went to visit Pepin, the King of the Franks. Pepin had been brought up by the monks of St. Denis near Paris and was a Christian ruler. He had fought against the Frisians and driven out their pagan king. He welcomed Willibrord gladly and gave him his royal

authority to preach to the Frisians, ordering that no one was to hinder the monks. Eagerly Willibrord and his friends set off to the Frisians. They were fierce people and had cruel ways, for their gods were evil and bloodthirsty. Some of the monks were put to death and became martyrs of the Church. But Willibrord went on bravely with his work and many Frisians gave up their idols and turned to the true God.

After three years Willibrord went to Rome. He wanted to win the support of the Pope for his missionary work. He wanted also to get relics of the saints and martyrs of old. For it was the custom in those days to have a relic of one of the saints in each new church. Then the church would be dedicated in the name of that saint. The heathens believed that their idols had great power. They worshipped gods made of wood and stone; sometimes they even worshipped a tree. To have a relic in church helped them to believe in the power of the saints. The Pope was glad to hear Willibrord tell of his work and gave him all the help and support he wanted. So the monks had the blessing of the Church as well as the authority of the King of the Franks.

Willibrord went back to the Frisians and lived among them in great happiness. Many pagans were baptised and churches were built. King Pepin took a great interest in this work. He realised that the Frisians needed a bishop of their own. He sent Willibrord to Rome, asking the Pope to make him Bishop of the Frisians. The Pope gave Willibrord his own special authority, making him Archbishop. This was in the year A.D. 695. It is the custom of the Church for each bishop to be known by the name of the place which is chosen for his seat. King Pepin made Willibrord the Archbishop of Utrecht, a city where the King had a famous castle. He gave him land, too, just outside the city, where he could build his cathedral. Thus Willibrord had a splendid centre for the missionary work he loved so well.

But Willibrord had been brought up in monasteries. He knew that he himself must have a monastery built right among the Frisians. There his monks could live, setting an example of holy living to the pagans. From it they could go out on their missionary journeys far and wide. So, three years later, he built his own monastery at a place called Echternach in the country called now Luxembourg. It became famous for the monks who

went out from it as missionaries to the heathen tribes of Europe.

Willibrord set up other monasteries, too, and built churches. From his monks he chose holy men whom he made bishops. Year by year the Church spread among the Frisian people. Their idols were cast down and destroyed; their fears of evil spirits disappeared. Slowly they learned to live in peace and brotherhood.

Willibrord himself was never content to stay at Utrecht. He went further afield each year, taking the Gospel of Jesus wherever he journeyed. He went deep into the forests of Germany; he visited the island of Heligoland and made his way as far as Denmark. Others followed in his footsteps so that when he died in A.D. 739 his work continued. November 7th was the day set aside to his memory in the Christian year.

It is strange that Willibrord, an Englishman, became the patron saint of Holland. But there is something even more important about him. He was an Anglo-Saxon. The stories in this book have shown how Christianity was brought to the pagan Angles and Saxons. Now they were taking the Gospel to others. Willibrord was the first missionary to go out from England and to win fame as the Apostle of the Netherlands.

Questions and Things To Do

1. Find and read these passages in your Bible which remind us of Willibrord—

    The call of the missionary   St. Matthew 28. vv. 19–20
    Witnesses of Jesus   Acts 1. v. 8
    The Christian way of life   Romans 12. vv. 10–14
    The man of God   1 Timothy 6. vv. 11–12.

2. Make your own map to illustrate the life of Willibrord, marking on it the places mentioned in this story.

3. The Latin word *cathedra* means a chair. It was the word used for the chair of a bishop from which he preached and ruled his people. The church in which his seat was placed came to be called a ' cathedral'. That is why we say that Willibrord had his 'seat' in the city of Utrecht. Write this meaning in your notebook.

4. Though nowadays we do not have relics in our churches, every church is named after a saint. Find out all you can about the saint to whom your church is dedicated and write an account of his life and work, illustrating it with drawings and pictures, too, if you can.

5. It seems strange to us that pagan people used to be afraid of evil spirits, for we know they do not exist. You can find an example of this belief in John Bunyan's great hymn—'Who would true valour see'. Read it through in choral speaking and see what it says about 'hobgoblins'. Make sure you know this fine 'Pilgrim Hymn' to use in school assembly.

6. In the Church of Willibrord there were three kinds of ministers—deacons, priests and bishops. The Church of England still has these three orders but some other Churches do not. Deacons and priests are 'ordained', bishops are 'consecrated', at special services. So we should say that Willibrord was 'consecrated' a bishop. Write this meaning in your notebook.

7. Why do you think Willibrord wanted to go as a missionary in Europe when missionaries were still needed in England?

8. Make up a service for Willibrord's Day, choosing hymns, a lesson and prayers which you think suitable.

9. Make up a prayer for missionaries in other lands who carry on the work of Willibrord.

10. What kind of person do you think a missionary should be? When you have talked about this, make a list of the qualities which a missionary must possess to do his work.

★

18. Boniface, Apostle of Germany

IN the year A.D. 680 a son was born to the Saxon thane of Crediton, a village in Devon. He was given the name 'Winfrith' from which our word 'winsome' comes. It means one full of joy and peace. Crediton was in the great Kingdom of Wessex and the thane was a nobleman for he came from the King's family. The people of Wessex had become Christians and the King himself was a devout man. The thane welcomed travellers to his wooden house in Crediton and especially the monks. On winter nights the whole household gathered in the hall to eat and drink and to tell stories. The boy Winfrith loved these evenings, especially when travellers told of the exciting world beyond the quiet village. One night, when Winfrith was five years old, some monks arrived. After supper they told of their travels. Winfrith sat by the blazing fire eagerly listening. They had been across the sea to the land of Frisia, now called Holland. They told of their adventures in preaching the Gospel to the fierce, pagan Frisians. Winfrith had never heard such exciting stories, and he never forgot them.

When he was seven years old, Winfrith went to school at the monastery of Exminster, near Exeter. He was a clever scholar and a hard worker. He grew up strong in body, too, a tall fair-haired Saxon. But more important to him than anything else was his love for God and his

desire to be a missionary. After some years he went to a famous Abbey at a place called Nursling near Winchester. He became a good scholar, able to read and write in Latin and to read the Gospels in Greek. The monks agreed that he would be the obvious choice for their next Abbot.

But Winfrith had never forgotten the stories he had heard the monks tell of the heathen tribes in Europe. In his heart he longed to follow in their footsteps. In the year A.D. 716 his chance came. He and three friends set off from the monastery. They trudged along the dusty lanes to London and there took ship in a little wooden boat across the sea. They landed safely in Frisia but soon they were safe no more. Rathbod, the heathen King of the Frisians, was at war with the King of the Franks. His

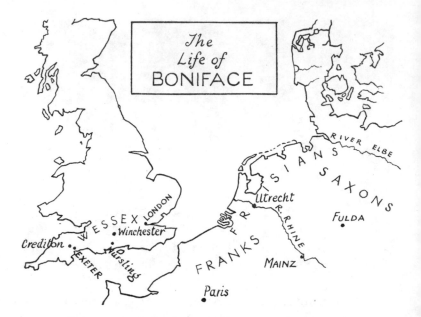

The
Life of
BONIFACE

name was Charles Martel and he was a great Christian warrior. It was he who drove back the dreaded followers of Mohammed the Prophet and stopped them from conquering Europe. Winfrith hoped to join the famous missionary Willibrord. But he found churches destroyed and villages burned by fire in the bitter fighting. Bravely he went to see the Frisian King himself. But Rathbod hated Christians and he told Winfrith to leave his country. The monks sailed sadly back to England.

But Winfrith refused to give up. It was about this time that he took a new name, Boniface. It came from two Latin words and it meant, 'One who does good'. He determined to live up to his name. In A.D. 718 he set off again. First he travelled on foot across France on the way to Rome to win the support of the Pope. Pope Gregory II liked the eager Saxon monk and gladly gave Boniface his own authority to work as a missionary. Boniface hurried back to Frisia. On his way he heard that King Rathbod was dead, which meant that he and his monks would be able to preach freely. He went by boat down the River Rhine till he came to Utrecht. There at last he met his missionary hero, the famous Willibrord. He was an old man by that time and wanted Boniface to stay with him and carry on his work. But the keen Saxon wanted to go where no Christian had been before. He journeyed deep into Germany where lived Saxon tribes who, like the Frisians, were kinsmen to his own people in England. So he was able to speak to them in their own language. He was one of them and soon his preaching bore fruit. The Pope heard of his excellent work and called him to Rome. He made Boniface bishop of all the tribes who lived to the east of the River Rhine and he asked the King of the Franks to help Boniface in his great work.

A well-known story is told of how Boniface won the pagans to the Christian faith. Near a place called Fritzlar there stood a famous oak tree called 'The Thunderer's Oak', for it was sacred to the chief of the Saxon gods, Woden, from whose name comes our 'Wednesday' or 'Woden's day'. Boniface called the people together round the sacred tree and told them he was going to cut it down. Some of the pagans were angry and others frightened. Boniface realised that if he felled the tree he would show that their god had no power and that he did not

exist. With sturdy blows from his axe he cut down the tree which was old and hollow. From it his monks made a small wooden shrine for the worship of the true God.

Boniface did not often do things like that. He always looked for what was good in the heathen religion. He wanted the pagans to find out for themselves how silly it was to believe in spirits of trees and rivers and mountains and to bow down before idols of wood and stone. He wrote many letters back to England about his work. From the monasteries came books and clothes and vessels for the little wooden churches which sprang up over the land. Some nuns came out to help him, led by his cousin Leoba. Monasteries were set up as centres for the missionary monks. In A.D. 747 the Pope made Boniface Archbishop of Mainz, a city on the Rhine, and six other bishops were consecrated to help him.

A few years later Boniface gave up his work at Mainz and went to spend his last years among his beloved Frisians. There in the year A.D. 755 he and his monks were killed by a band of warriors. June 5th, the day of their martyrdom, was set aside in the Christian year as a memorial to Boniface, the great-hearted Saxon missionary, the Apostle of Germany.

Questions and Things To Do

1. Find and read in your Bible these passages which remind us of Boniface—

    The call of the missionary   St. Mark 16. v. 15
    The greatest love   St. John 15. v. 13
    Faithful unto death   Revelation 2. v. 10.

2. Make your own map to illustrate the life of Boniface, marking on it the places mentioned in this story.

3. There are several exciting events in the story for you to draw. Illustrate the life of Boniface in a series of drawings as a strip cartoon.

4. Boniface met his death in a camp which he and his monks had made by a river. He was waiting to take a confirmation service when the savages attacked them. Just before he died he quoted to his monks the words of Jesus in St. Matthew 10. v. 28. Find this verse in your Bible. What do you think it means?

5. Boniface was a fine organiser. He divided up the land of the German tribes and put a bishop in charge of each part. The district a bishop looks after is called 'a diocese'. The Pope also asked Boniface to do the same for the land of the Franks. Find out about the organisation of your own church and write or tell the story of what you find.

6. Boniface was buried in the monastery he himself had founded at Fulda in Germany where his body still lies in the Abbey Church. Make up a service which could be used at Fulda on St. Boniface Day, choosing your own lesson and hymns and prayers.

7. When Boniface came back to his monastery after his first vain journey to Frisia, the monks were glad. They thought it foolish to have risked his life among savages. Besides, their old Abbot was dying and they wanted Boniface in his place. But Boniface refused. Act this scene, using your own words to tell what you think the monks and Boniface said to each other.

8. Imagine you were a Saxon boy or girl standing by your sacred oak tree when Boniface cut it down. Describe in your own words what happened, what you think Boniface may have said, and what your people felt about it.

9. Find out from your reference books all you can about Saxons, their homes, their dress, their customs and manners. Make a model of the home of Boniface at Crediton or write an account of his life there.

10. Compare Boniface with Willibrord whom you read about in the last story. In what ways were they alike? In what ways were they different?

★

19. Anskar, Apostle of the North

ANSKAR was born in the year A.D. 801 at a place named Corbie near Amiens, now a city in France. In those days Corbie lay in the realm of the King of the Franks named Charlemagne. Anskar's father worked in the royal court. He and his wife were Germans and they had become Christians through the work of the famous missionary Boniface. When he was a boy, Anskar heard many stories of the great saint and even then he may have wanted to become a missionary like him.

When Anskar was five years old his mother died. His father sent him to the school of the monastery at Corbie which was renowned for its many precious books and its good teaching. Anskar was a rough and mischievous boy till one night he dreamed of his mother whom he barely remembered. She gently chided him for his folly and, when he awoke, Anskar determined to follow her gentle goodness. He became a serious boy, devoted to his studies and above all to the service of God. When he was old enough he became a monk at Corbie. He became such a fine scholar that it was not long before he was called to a monastery in Germany. It was at a place called Mayence and it had been founded by Boniface. Anskar was to look after the monastery school and he did his work well. But he had never lost his desire to be a missionary.

In the year A.D. 826 his chance came. Harold, the King of Denmark, came on a visit to Germany. Charlemagne had built up a great empire and now his son Louis was the Emperor of Germany. Like his father, Louis was a good Christian and it was not long before the King of Denmark asked to be baptised. Then he asked the Emperor for a missionary to take back with him to Denmark to preach to his people. Louis sent for the Abbot of Mayence. "Is there anyone brave enough to undertake this work?" he asked. "Yes!" replied the Abbot. "I have in my monastery a monk named Anskar. He is full of courage and of faith. He longs to be a missionary." The Emperor sent for Anskar and at once he eagerly agreed to go to Denmark.

The monks at Mayence were astonished. Anskar was

giving up everything to risk his life among the fierce Northmen. They had never heard of Christ and in every land people dreaded the terrible Vikings as they were called. They were bold seafarers who feared no sea and no man in their swift longboats. They came from the flat, sandy waterways of Denmark, from the islands of Sweden and from the towering fjords of Norway. They came sometimes as traders but mostly as pirates. They plundered and destroyed and killed. In Christian lands a new prayer was added to the litany of the Church: "From the fury of the Northmen, good Lord, deliver us." To the monks it was madness for Anskar to go and live among such savages. To Anskar it was the call of God.

Anskar was delighted when his friend Autbert, the Prior of the monastery, asked to go with him. They went by land to Cologne with King Harold and his courtiers. The Bishop of Cologne gave Anskar a small boat and in that he sailed round Holland to Denmark. At once he started a school, the very first in the lands of the Vikings. After two years Autbert fell ill and had to go back home. Then the pagan Danes attacked Anskar. King Harold had angered them by trying to force them to give up the gods of their forefathers. Anskar was compelled to return home.

Anskar had barely reached his monastery when an urgent summons came from the Emperor. Messengers from Sweden wanted a Christian missionary in their land. Would he go? Anskar felt it was the call of God and immediately set off. He and his friend Witmar, a monk, sailed in a trading-ship with their belongings and their precious books. But near the coast of Sweden the ship was attacked by pirates and they were lucky to escape with their lives. They had lost everything else. But Anskar was undaunted. They trudged through the snow till they came to the court of King Biorn and won his consent to their preaching. For two years Anskar laboured in Sweden, teaching the Gospel of Jesus and building the first churches. There were some Christian slaves in the land who helped his work, but progress was slow. Anskar never gave up for he knew that even great things have tiny beginnings.

In A.D. 832 the Pope made Anskar Bishop of Hamburg. This made him in charge of all missionary work in these

northern countries. He could seize any opportunity that came. His nephew was made Bishop of Sweden to carry on his work there. Anskar himself was determined to go back to Denmark. The Christian King Harold had died and a fierce Viking named Horick ruled the land. Anskar had no fear of him. He went to Denmark as an ambassador of the Emperor. By patient love he won the respect of King Horick and he was allowed to build churches and to preach. He showed his greatest love to the many slaves whom the Danes had captured and worked hard to make their lives happier.

The fame of Anskar spread far and wide and in A.D. 848 the Pope made him the first Archbishop of Bremen. He had to leave others to continue his work in Denmark. But it was not long before sad news came from Sweden.

The bishop had been driven out and the new King, named Olaf, would have nothing to do with the Christian God. Anskar sailed again to Sweden. His friends warned him of the danger. "I am quite ready to die for the sake of Jesus," he replied simply. He invited King Olaf and his nobles to a banquet. Olaf decided to call a council and there it was agreed to allow the Christians to teach about their God.

Anskar laboured on till his death in A.D. 865. February 3rd was set aside as his feast day for the church to remember this heroic Apostle of the North.

Questions and Things To Do

1. Find and read in your Bible these passages which remind us of Anskar—

    Following in the steps of Jesus St. Mark 1. vv. 14–15
    Facing persecution St. Matthew 5. vv. 10–12
    The family of God Acts 17. vv. 26–27
    Building the Church Ephesians 2. vv. 19–22.

2. Make your own map of northern Europe to illustrate the life and work of Anskar, marking on it the places mentioned in this story.

3. Use your reference books to find out all you can about the Vikings, their ships, their dress, their customs and their ways. Imagine you were a boy or girl in a village on the east coast of England when the Vikings came. Describe what they were like and what happened. You can illustrate your story with drawings of Viking ships and warriors.

4. Christians added to their litany a new prayer about the North-men. 'Litany' comes from a Greek word meaning 'prayer of asking'. It is a special kind of prayer in which the people join all through. The minister said a short 'petition' or 'asking' and the people made the 'response'. Thus the priest said "From the fury of the Northmen" and the people answered "Good Lord, deliver us". You can find the Litany in the Prayer Book of the Church of England and read parts of it in this way.

5. After Anskar's death the north lands became pagan again. His work seemed a failure. But he was never forgotten. Later, King Canute of England, who was himself a Dane, sent missionaries to these lands which he had conquered. Find out about this from your reference books and describe King Canute and his work.

6. What example can you give from this story of the courage of Anskar? Do you think he was brave or foolhardy? Why do you think he had such courage?

7. Anskar felt called by God to do this work in Denmark and Sweden. How do you think he knew this? In what ways does God call us?

8. Read together in choral speaking the Psalm which you think might have been Anskar's favourite—for example, Psalms 31, 46 or 67. Say why you chose it.

9. There are several exciting scenes in this story for you to draw. Tell the life story of Anskar in a series of pictures as a strip cartoon.

10. Anskar never gave up even when he had little success and his work seemed a failure. What do you think we can learn from this as Christians?

★

20. Vladimir, Apostle of Russia

OUR final story takes us far away from the world of the West to Russia in the East. There, too, the Church was growing. We have seen how in the West the Church spread from the great city of Rome. For the Bishop of Rome had become head of the Church. In the same way the Church in the East spread from the great city of Constantinople and the Bishop there was its head. Constantine, the first Roman Emperor to be a Christian, had founded this city. From Constantinople the monks went out as missionaries among the pagan tribes called the Slavs. The Slavs had no alphabet or writing so the monks made one, using Greek letters. Then they translated their Bible and their prayer-book so that the Slavs could worship God in their own language. Slowly the tribes were won to Christianity.

While some Northmen invaded the lands of the West, others went to the East. One of their leaders, named Rurik, chose a place called Kiev to settle in and he founded a kingdom there. It was the beginning of Russia. His son named Igor married a beautiful Viking lady called Olga and she went to live with him in Kiev. There she first heard of the Christian faith. For in a little church there, monks from Constantinople taught the Gospel of Jesus. They told Olga of the wonderful city from which they had come and of the glorious cathedral there. Olga decided to visit this fine place. She travelled by boat down the River Dnieper and then across the Black Sea till she came to Constantinople. It was even more wonderful than she had dreamt. The cathedral, built 400 years before, glittered in the sunlight. Its marble pillars had been brought from the Far East and they were rich in colour—green and

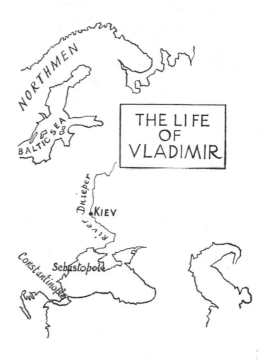

purple, red and white. The great building soared up to the skies, crowned with high domes. Inside, beautiful pictures in stone covered the walls; the altars glittered with gold and silver and precious stones. Olga remained in the lovely city, learning the Christian faith. Then in the year A.D. 957, she was baptised by the great Bishop of Constantinople himself.

Olga took a priest back with her to Kiev to teach her people. When her husband died, her son became ruler. But he did not care for his mother's religion and spent much of his time away from his home fighting. His little

139

son Vladimir, born in A.D. 956, was brought up by his grandmother Olga. She told him many stories of Jesus and of great Christian heroes. She told him, too, of the wonders of Constantinople and its beautiful cathedral. She hoped that Vladimir would grow up into a fine Christian ruler. But he showed himself fierce and cruel. He wanted to be a tyrant and to have great power. He seized Kiev and other lands left to his brothers by their father. He fought against other rulers and conquered them till he had built himself a great kingdom. He lived by the sword and made his kingdom rich by trade with other lands.

Vladimir had no religion of his own. On his campaigns he met Moslems, followers of Mohammed the Prophet. But their God seemed a powerful tyrant and Vladimir wanted none of him. He met Jews and despised them because they had lost their homeland. He met Christians from Rome but he wanted no Pope lording it over him. He met monks from Constantinople and their words reminded him of the stories his grandmother told him as a boy. Then he sent his noblemen to visit the churches of all these people. When they came back, Vladimir called a council to listen to their reports. None of them interested him till those who had been to Constantinople told of its glories. "In the cathedral we felt we were in heaven," they said. "Words cannot describe its glory. Truly God must dwell there. For our part we cannot believe in our pagan gods any more." Then Vladimir made up his mind.

But he was too proud to seek baptism meekly. He led his army against a city now called Sebastopol. It belonged

to the Greek Emperors. "If I conquer it, I will be baptised," he said. It soon fell to his host and Vladimir was baptised in Constantinople with great splendour, just as he intended. Then he gave back the city to the two Greek Emperors who ruled at that time, on condition that they gave him their sister in marriage. Princess Anna was a good Christian. She agreed to marry Vladimir and went back with him to Kiev. She hoped she could persuade her wild and proud husband to make his people Christian.

Vladimir took some monks back with him to teach his people. But even in making them Christians he had to show his power. He made a royal decree ordering his people to meet by the River Dnieper. "Those who do not go into the water to be baptised will be my enemies," he

proclaimed. So he forced his people to enter the Church. That was very foolish and wrong. Vladimir did not understand that God wants men to come to him by love, never by force.

Vladimir always remained a proud tyrant. But it was through him that the missionary monks from Constantinople were able to go through his kingdom setting up schools and churches in towns and villages. In the schools children were taught to read and write and then they could read themselves the fine Slav Bible made by the monks long before. Vladimir had a big stone cathedral built in Kiev, his capital city. In his later years he became more gentle through the good influence of his Queen Anna. He came to see that goodness and learning are finer than war and bloodshed. After his death in A.D. 1015 he was remembered as the ruler who had brought Christianity to Russia. He was made a saint of the Church and July 15th was set aside as a memorial to him. For, though he had many faults, he was the first Apostle of Russia.

Questions and Things To Do

1. Find and read in your Bible these passages which remind us of Vladimir—

A king builds a cathedral	1 Kings 8. vv. 12–13
A psalm of the house of God	Psalm 122. vv. 1–9
The temple of God	1 Corinthians 3. vv. 11, 16

2. Make your own map of Russia to illustrate the life of Vladimir, marking on it the places mentioned in this story.

3. Use reference books to find out all you can about the city of Constantinople and write a short history of it, with illustrations if you can. In the story of John Chrysostom you will find more about this great city.

4. We need to have churches for the worship of God and want them to be as beautiful as possible. But read carefully the words of Paul to the men of Athens in Acts 17. vv. 24–27. What do you think he meant by these words?

5. Why was Vladimir so wrong in forcing his people to become Christians?

6. The story of Vladimir was written by a Russian monk named Nestor. It was the first history book of Russia, just as the monk Bede's chronicle was the first history of England. Imagine you were Nestor the monk. Why did he think that Vladimir had done such a great work for Russia?

7. Use reference books to find out all you can about Mohammed the Prophet and what he taught. His religion is called 'Islam', an Arabic word meaning 'submission', for he taught that men must submit to God in everything. His followers are called 'Moslems' from the same word. Write an account of their religion.

8. From the time when it had the first Slav Bible, the Church in Russia has always taught the importance of reading the Scriptures. For what reasons do you think we should read the Bible? How does it help us? How and when do you think we should read it?

9. Imagine you were one of the monks whom Vladimir took back to his kingdom. Describe what he was like, what he did, and what work you did in Russia.

10. All the saints you have read about in this book have a special day set aside in the Christian year to their memory. Make a list of them all and work out a 'Calendar of Saints' of all those in this book. You can add to it other Saints' days you may know, if you wish.

★